LEFTY'S LITTLE FLY-FISHING TIPS

200 Innovative Ideas
For Improving Your Fly Fishing

LEFTY KREH

THE LYONS PRESS
Guilford, Connecticut
An imprint of The Globe Pequot Press

The Lyons Press is an imprint of The Globe Pequot Press.

10 9 8 7 6 5 4 3 2

Printed in China
ISBN: 1-58574-629-0

The Library of Congress Cataloguing-in-Publication Data is available on file.

CONTENTS

INTRODUCTION

One of the most enjoyable aspects of fishing — especially fly fishing — is that as the sport progresses over time, so many neat ideas are continuously being conceived or invented. These new concepts not only make things easier for us, but also make the sport more enjoyable. Oftentimes, these little tips also help us with the practical side of fishing — by preserving our tackle longer, for example, which saves us money (always a pleasurable experience). More importantly, they frequently help us in becoming more skilled and successful fly fishermen.

The following tips are ones either that I have come up with over the years, or that friends and fishing buddies have shared with me. I offer all of them to you here in my little book — help yourself. I'm sure that many of them will make your fly fishing more fun.

OPPOSITE: *Lefty on a Florida Keys flat, selecting a fly he hopes will catch a bonefish. A summer trout vest is cool and ideal for carrying fly boxes and other necessities. See Tip Number 159 for the proper method of wading the flats.* OVERLEAF: *Fly rods rigged for the morning's fishing at an Alaskan fly-out lodge. See Tips Number 1-31 for advice on reels, rods, and lines.*

CHAPTER ONE

TACKLE TIPS

RODS

1. COLOR CODE YOUR TRAVEL RODS — Several years ago I went to the Bahamas, taking five of the new four-piece travel rods with me. When I came home and unpacked, I realized that I had 20 rod sections and no idea which pieces mated with which. I decided at that point to mark my rods so that I would never run into this problem again.

Using small bottles of enamel hobby paint (I used Testor's PLA), I put a colored dot on each rod section, using blue for 8-weight rods, orange for 7s, white for 6s, and so on. After painting the dots on, I sprayed each with a little clear gloss enamel to protect the paint.

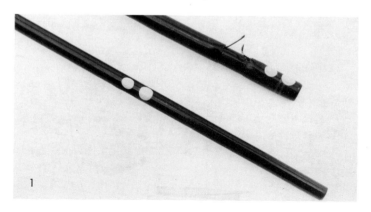

1

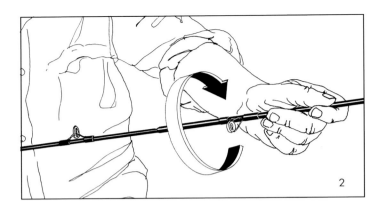

2. CORRECTLY PUTTING A ROD TOGETHER — At some time while casting, almost all fly fishermen have had their rod tip fall off. The reason is that anglers commonly assemble a rod by holding the two pieces near eye level, and when all guides are aligned, they'll shove the two parts of the rod together. That's the whole problem!

Instead, the tip section should be held so that its guides are positioned about 90 degrees from the angle of the other rod section to which it will be joined. Then, the male section of the rod should be inserted into the female section, and as the two pieces are brought together, the tip section should be turned at final closure. All guides are now aligned, and your rod will rarely come apart.

3. LUBRICATING RODS — Another reason for rod tips falling off during casting C and it happens with all types of rods C fly, plug, or spinning C is because when the male section of the ferrule becomes very dry, the tip tends to work itself free and will eventually fall off.

In order to prevent this from happening, the male section should be lubricated every now and then. Some anglers use paraffin for the job, but this kind of wax soon

wears off. Beeswax is also sometimes used, but it tends to be tacky and can pick up dirt, which can erode the ferrule.

The best thing I know to use is a candle which has a wax with just enough of an oily base to lubricate well and still not be tacky. So, just rub a candle on the male section of the ferrule every now and then. I carry a small birthday candle in my fly fishing vest, in case I need it in the field.

4. CHECK THOSE GUIDES — Ceramic rod guides can get chipped or develop small cracks, which are even more difficult to detect. Such damage can really harm a fly line, so

you need to check for even the finest cracks or chips in your rod guides.

Do this by either drawing a cotton Q-Tip or a section of nylon pantyhose through the guide. Using either of these methods, if there is a nick or crack in a rod guide, you will be able immediately to detect it when it snags on the soft material.

5. ROD REEL SEATS — There are two basic reel seat designs on most fly rods.

Shown on the left below is a down-locking seat. When the reel is put on this kind of seat, the tightening rings are screwed downward to capture the reel. But I prefer the up-locking seat, shown on the right, because it has two advantages over the down-locking design. An up-locking seat will give you a short rod butt extension to stick in your stomach when fighting a large fish; and, more importantly, your hand won't tend to loosen the rings when casting — a major disadvantage of down-locking seats.

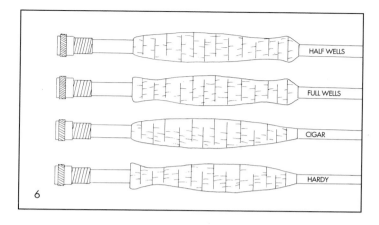

6

6. ROD HANDLES — Fly rod handles come in different shapes. The two most popular are the half-Wells and full-Wells designs. Both these handles offer the caster an advantage over other types of handles. Since correct casting technique requires that the thumb should rest at the top of the handle, the half and full-Wells designs allow the angler to push his thumb against the handle when he accelerates the rod at the end of the cast.

Cigar-shaped handles are rarely found on the heavier fly rods that are used for long distance casting. However, many smaller rods come equipped with the cigar design because "cosmetically" they look nice. The Hardy design is considered by most experienced anglers to be better than the cigar-shape handle, but neither is as effective or comfortable as the half and full-Wells designs.

7. COMFORTABLE BUTT EXTENSIONS — When fighting strong fish, the angler has to stick the end or butt of the rod against his stomach. I would suggest using one of the three butt extensions pictured on the right on the next page. All have rounded edges and feel more comfortable. The butt

7

extension pictured on the left is really less desirable, since in a long fight its sharp edges would become very uncomfortable against the stomach.

8. SLIDE THAT ROD IN THE TUBE — There are times when you may find that one of the snake guides of your rod has a loose foot. This can often happen if the rod bag is just

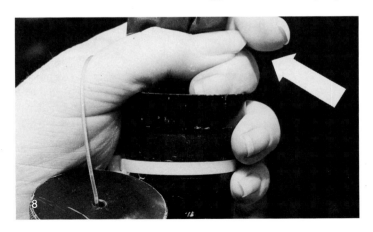

8

slipped and released into the tube. When it is carelessly released in this way, the snake guides of the rod sections may strike against the side of the tube and be pulled loose. In order to prevent this, enclose your fingers gently around the rod bag and slide it slowly down inside the tube.

9. CAPTURE THE CAP — It's so easy to lose a rod tube cap — ask almost any fly fisherman. To eliminate the problem, drill a small hole in the center of the cap. Then, insert a length of 60 to 100-pound monofilament through the hole, and on the inside of the cap, tie off a knot. I seal the knot by lighting it with a match, which will prevent it from ever unravelling.

Then secure a tie wrap (a thin nylon strap that when pulled tight will lock into position), around the upper end of the rod case (as shown in photo). Slip the monofilament under the tie wrap, making sure to tie another knot on the end to prevent it from slipping free, and draw the tie wrap very tight. Be sure to trim the end of the tie wrap and then add a drop or two of hot glue or epoxy to prevent it from sliding down the tube.

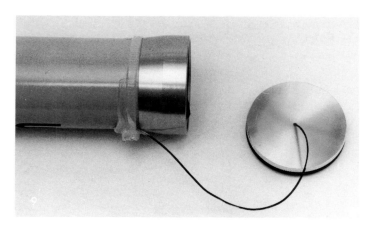

10. SHORTEN THE ROD TIP — Many experienced fly fishermen have removed a fly rod from its aluminum rod tube and found that the top of the tip was crooked. They will bend the tip back into its proper position, only to discover the next time they remove the rod from the tube, it has become crooked again. This time when the tip top is bent back into its proper position, it is likely to break.

This happens because many rod tubes are simply too short for the rod sections they were designed to accommodate, and the tip of the rod can become jammed against the tube cap when it is screwed tight in closing. To eliminate this problem, you can simply remove the metal tip guide and a small portion of the tip so that the rod will fit comfortably into the tube. Shorten the rod tip about 3/4-inch by cutting it with a razor blade around the circumference of the tip. Be sure to save the metal tip guide from this piece you have cut off. When you need to reinstall the tip guide, heat it, add a little glue, and then re-attach it to the rod. The rod will now be as good as new. And this short reduction in the length of your rod will not affect your casting in any way. (Not illustrated.)

11. STABLE CASES — You may use a rod case that can be adjusted lengthwise for carrying several rods at a time. On this type case, if the adjustment lock breaks or fails, the top of the carrying case may collapse onto your rods and most likely break them. To avoid this problem, purchase a length of 1/2-inch plastic pipe from a local hardware or plumbing shop. Cut the pipe so that it is about one inch longer than the longest rod you are carrying or shipping. The plastic pipe should fit nicely into the rod case. Now if the adjustment lock fails, the carrying case will collapse onto the plastic pipe without being able to travel further down and hit your rods. (Not illustrated.)

12

12. NON-SLIP ROD CASE — Almost all rod tubes have a slippery, smooth bottom, so when stored upright, they slide and topple over. To prevent this, cut a piece of rubber gasket material (I use inner tubes from old tires) and glue it to the bottom of the tube.

13. ONE OF THE BEST TRAVEL ROD CASES — Pictured below (in both closed and opened positions) is one of the best travel rod cases that allows you to store rods, rain gear,

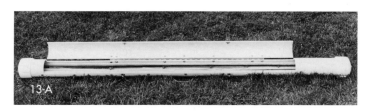

13-A

13-B

and any other clothing. Unlike the conventional travel tube in which you can only insert gear in one end, this one lets you pack things in both ends. To make one, saw out a section from one end of a travel case and install a long piano hinge on one side. On the other *interior* edge of the pipe, pop rivet a thin piece of 1/8 x 3/4-inch aluminum strapping. When you close the door of the tube, its face should rest against the aluminum strap. Install clasps, as shown, or use a simpler method of securing the hinged door by putting two large flexible clamps around the tube.

14. LABEL ROD BAGS — Most fly fishermen now carry two to four rods on trips. Each rod usually comes with an individual manufacturer's cloth bag. To be sure you have the correct bag for each rod, affix a label made from a short length of masking tape to each bag. Then, write the line weight and length of the rod on the label. *(Not illustrated.)*

15. PUT A HANDLE ON IT — Round rod cases are difficult to hold, especially while traveling when you are loaded down with the rod case plus several pieces of baggage. But you can install a simple handle that costs less than

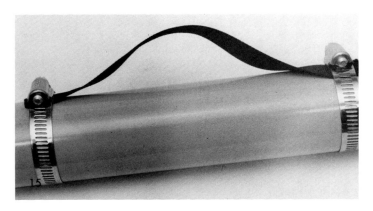

two dollars in just a few minutes. Buy two stainless steel adjustable clamps of the same size, and install them on the case at a balance point with a piece of rope or strapping. This kind of strap will not only help you to carry the case, but will also prevent it from rolling around in the car.

16. MY FAVORITE TRAVEL ROD CASE — Many traveling fly fishermen are now using the longer fly rods designed in three or four sections. The relatively short rod case that is provided with these rods allows you to take your rods aboard the plane with your other carry-on bags, insuring that when you arrive at your destination, your rods will have arrived with you. But many people then will turn around and pack their reels and flies in their suitcase for loading on the plane as checked baggage. Instead, I suggest that you purchase a case that also has room for the rest of your tackle. My favorite is a case with a large pouch constructed along one of its sides. In such a case as this, you can store reels, flies, leaders, pliers, etc., plus your rods, which means that everything you need for fly fishing will be traveling with you at all times, no matter where the airline sends your checked baggage.

17

17. READY TO GO AND OUT OF THE WAY — If you or someone you know is handy with a sewing machine, you can easily make these bags, using long socks made of light nylon which are enlarged on the open end. Your fly rods can be fully rigged in these bags, protecting the rigging of each rod from becoming tangled with other rods while you are in transit in boat or car. Several rods matched with different sink rate lines, floating or sinking lines, or with various fly patterns, can in this way all be ready-rigged and available for casting within a few minutes. Then at the end of your fishing day, if you do not have your permanent rod cases with you, you can disassemble the pieces and store them temporarily in these same bags.

18. VELCRO CAPTURES ROD — If you would like to carry your rod already assembled in the car or boat and want a super-quick way to keep it in place, try Joy Hilliard's

trick. Take two pieces of Velcro and snap a piece together on each end of the rod. The rod is held together, and the tabs can be stored in your fishing jacket when not in use.

19. HOW TO CARRY A ROD THROUGH THE WOODS —
After you have broken your first fly rod and have to buy your second, you will probably have learned never to carry a rod through the woods with the tip extended in front of you. But even a rod carried behind you can create problems. Sometimes the line exiting from the reel, as well as the line and leader lying along the rod blank, can get caught on brush.

To avoid this, pull off enough line and leader so that you can insert the hook in a guide located two or three inches back from the tip. Then bring the leader back and around the handle of the rod, just behind the reel, which will result in the leader lying flat along the rod. Then wind in any ex-

cess line, grasp the leader at the first butt or stripper guide, and wind it several times around the guide. Now all of the line and leader will be stored right next to the rod blank and cannot tangle in brush.

20. NEVER PUT IT ON THE ROOF— Often when anglers return to the car and get out of their fishing clothes, they will lay their tackle on the roof of the car. Then they will get in the car and drive away, forgetting about the gear and generally losing it. I did this with some of the first flies I ever tied. Since then, I've learned never to place anything on the roof of a car or lean anything against a car door. If you must put something down, always place it on the hood, where you can't fail to see it as you are beginning to drive away. (Not illustrated.)

A nice smallmouth bass caught on a rabbit fur fly. ➤

21. LEATHER RIM CONTROL — Some fly reels have an exposed rim on the handle side. As a fish pulls line from the reel in attempting to escape, the angler can place his fingers against the smooth, revolving rim to restrict the fish's progress. But damp fingers will often dry under the friction caused by contact with the revolving spool rim which, in turn, will sometimes cause enough jerky drag pressure to break a fragile leader.

To solve this problem, cut a small paddle shape from an old leather belt and lash it to the post supporting the side frames.

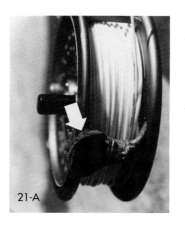

Now when the fish runs, you can apply smooth pressure on the rim by pushing lightly against the leather tab. I have used tabs like this for years of hard service.

22. MODIFYING A REEL — Many anglers don't have the money to spend on a fancy saltwater reel with a superb drag, even though they would like to pursue the great

saltwater species that require this kind of tackle. But you can modify many inexpensive reels with a simple trick that will permit you to have enough drag to control even rather large fish.

Remove the spool from the reel, and with a metal-cutting saber saw, cut out a section of the side plate as illustrated in photo 22-A. Be careful you don't saw any vital parts of the reel. Smooth the cut edges and paint the exposed area. Reinstall the spool and you are ready.

When a big fish makes its run, place your thumb inside the cut-out area and press against the spool to obtain the pressure you think you need (22-B). You can easily control even a very large fish in this manner.

22-A   22-B   22-C

Most of these inexpensive reels have a single handle, which can wobble on a high-speed run by a large fish. You can prevent this by attaching a 1/4 x 20-inch stainless steel thread nut in a position exactly opposite the reel handle, using epoxy glue (22-C).

23. THE BEST REEL STORAGE BAG — There are all sorts of bags for storing reels, but I favor this design over all others. This bag is flat at the top and rounded at the base. The cover fits over from the top, closed by a Velcro tab, so there is enough space between the flap and the top of the bag to hold an assembled rod together with reel, line, leader and fly. Another advantage of this type bag is that it can be

used as a separate storage bag to protect the reel while you are traveling.

LINES

24. MARKING FLY LINES — Fly lines are supplied with a label which should be attached to the spool holding the line. The trouble is that sometimes either the label falls off the spool or the line is used with another spool.

It is really important to mark the line, not the spool. Here's a method I have been using for more than 25 years. With a permanent marking pen, place a one-inch mark around the line approximately a foot up from the nail knot. That will be the mark for the number five. To signify a mark for the number one, make a small ring (approximately 1/4 inch-long) around the line with the pen. To further identify your lines by taper, for weight-forward lines

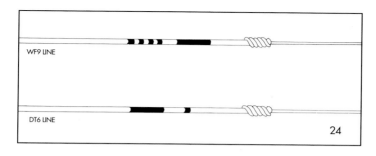

WF9 LINE

DT6 LINE

24

you can put the long mark forward of the line and the small ones toward the back. Thus (as shown on the line at the top of the illustration above), a weight-forward 9 weight line will have a one-inch mark forward of the line and four short ones toward the back.

For double-taper lines, simply reverse the process. Thus, a double-taper 6 weight line (as shown) would have one 1/4 inch-long mark forward of the line and a one-inch mark toward the back.

25. MARKING SPOOLS — For quicker identification, extra spools should be marked along with the lines that they hold. I've tried many ways, but the best material for mark-

25

ing a spool for any length of time is ordinary masking tape. Use either a graphite pencil or a thin-point permanent marking pen to write the line size and taper on the tape.

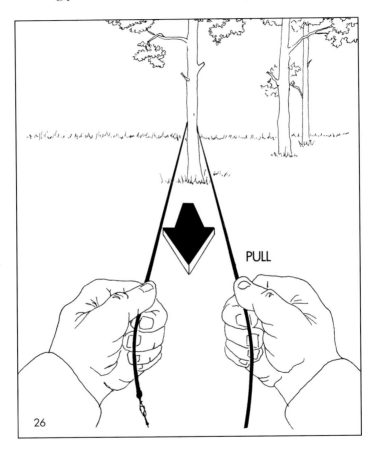

26. REMOVING THE CURLS FROM FLY LINES — Because most floating fly lines have a braided nylon core and are kept on a reel in small, tight coils, the line tends to take on the position in which it was last stored.

As a result, when you first strip off line to begin fishing, you'll note that the line lies before you in coils, so that when you cast and shoot it, the line tangles and spoils your presentation.

Stretching the line first to eliminate the coils will prevent such problems. If you have a companion, have him take the line and walk some distance with it. Then each of you should grip the line and give a steady pull. The appearance of the line will tell you when you have done the job.

If you are alone, slip the line around a stump, log, window post of a car door (or any other fixed object that is smooth enough not to cut the line), then pull firmly on both ends to stretch out the coils. Or if nothing else is available, pull off line and stretch it between your hands or slip the line under your foot, giving a stout pull on the line.

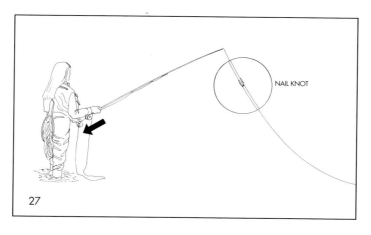

NAIL KNOT

27

27. MID-LINE NAIL KNOTS — Unless you are a highly skilled fly caster, there is an exact length of line extending outside the rod tip that is ideal for you to pick up and make the next cast with. If you bring in too much line, then you have to spend energy and time working out line by false

casting until you have the desired length. But if you leave more line outside the rod tip than you can comfortably pick up in one smooth motion, your cast can be spoiled.

To figure out exactly the amount of line you need to pick up, go out on a lawn and make a number of casts. Determine what length of line you can pick up easily. After some practice casts, make a forward cast of the length of line that you have found to be most comfortable for you, and make a mark on the line about one foot outside the rod tip. Then when you get back to your workbench, using 10 or 12-pound monofilament, tie a nail knot at the mark. Close the knot firmly so that it's solidly embedded in the line, then trim off the end neatly. As you retrieve a cast, the nail knot can be felt as it rides over your rod tip guide. When you feel the knot, just raise the rod and make your back cast — you know you have the right amount of line in the air.

28. DOUBLE THE LINE — As we get older, it becomes more difficult to see leader tippets. So never thread the leader end through the guides when stringing up your outfit. Instead, pull off about ten feet of line, then bend the line over about a foot behind where the leader butt is attached.

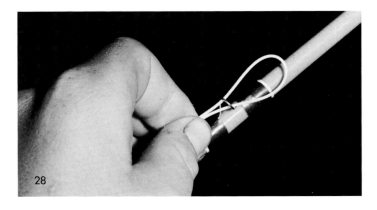

28

This doubled fly line can be clearly seen and can be passed through the rod guides very easily. And if your hands slip, the bent line loop won't fall back through the guides. While most anglers have learned this trick, many don't realize that once the loop has been pulled through the rod tip guide, it's not necessary to continue pulling the leader through the guides. You can simply make a quick flip of the rod and the leader will snake through on its own.

29. PULL OFF TO THE MARK — When you are fishing for tarpon, bonefish or permit, it is necessary to pull off the right amount of line you'll need to shoot the fly to the fish. But extra line lying on the deck of a boat can be real trouble, especially after the fish is hooked and is making a swift run. So it's a good idea not to pull off more line than you actually need. Make a cast at about 45 feet (it can be a little less or more depending upon your casting skill), then make a one-foot mark on your fly line just forward of the position where the line enters the reel. Now whenever you are stripping off line in preparation for making a cast, the mark will alert you when just the right amount of shooting line is available.

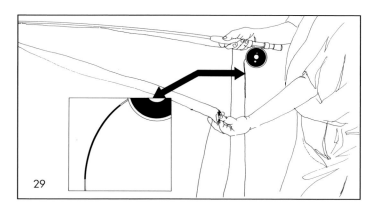

29

30. DYE THE FIRST 10 FEET — You can often catch more bonefish if you are able to make a long cast, as bonefish tend never to swim in the same direction for more than a few yards. If you wait until one gets very close and it changes direction just as you make your cast, you often don't have time for another shot.

But if you are a long caster, you can drop the fly at 60 or more feet in front of the fish. Then should the fish change direction, you have time to make a second cast, and often even a third. But knowing where the fly is at such a distance is difficult.

To help yourself in this situation, if you use a 10-foot leader, and you dye the last 10 feet of the fly line black, you will have a very good indicator. Black doesn't frighten bonefish, even on white flats. And it is a color that can be seen under almost all fishing conditions. With this device, as you make your long cast and the fish is approaching, you will know that 10 feet forward of the length of dyed line is where your fly will be.

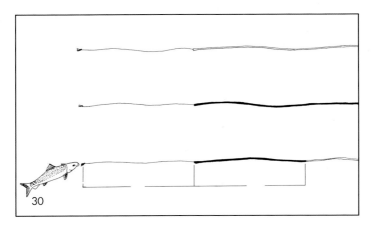

◄ *Dick Kreh fishing Big Hunting Creek, central Maryland.*

31. STORING IMPROPERLY — Sunlight and heat are wicked enemies of fly lines and other types of fishing lines. Never store your lines for any length of time in a car in warm weather. Heat and ultraviolet rays can actually ruin your lines. (*Not illustrated.*)

LEADERS

32. LOCATING THAT LEADER — Locating the tippet end of the leader after it has been wound on the spool is often difficult. It is very thin and hard to see. And when you get older, it seems to be even smaller.

There's a simple way to locate the leader end by using a large hook, usually a size 4 or larger. Carefully examine the spool and slip the hook under the thinnest strand of tippet you can see. Then start winding the reel handle as if you were retrieving line. Captured by the curve of the hook, the leader will chase around until it comes to the end.

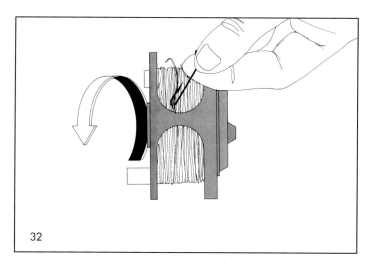

32

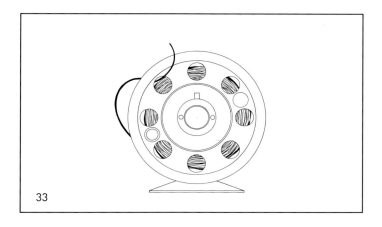

33

33. HIT THE HOLE — A bothersome task for anglers is trying to locate the end of a leader that has been wound on the reel. To eliminate the problem, if you are using a reel that has holes cut out of the spool — as do most small and intermediate-sized reels — wind in all but six inches of the leader end and insert it through one of the holes. Now turn the spool back and forth, and the leader end will remain captured. When you need the leader again for fishing, simply push it back through the hole.

34. STRAIGHTENING THE LEADER — Leaders are made from monofilament and will have a curl in them when removed from the spool. To cast accurately and get a good drift, the curls must be eliminated.

Never draw the monofilament leader through a section of rubber, since you take a good chance of scoring it. And any score or nick in a leader can drastically reduce its strength. Also, drawing a leader through a piece of rubber causes friction, generating heat that will often ruin it.

Instead, straighten the leader using your bare hands. Hold the leader inside a clenched fist, and while lightly

34

gripping it, drag the leader through the hand. If you feel discomfort, you are clenching it too tightly and building up destructive heat.

35. STORING LEADERS THE EASY WAY — Most leader material comes on spools provided with various devices to capture and store the leader end. However, there is a foolproof method of storing leaders that I prefer.

Drill two holes, approximately 1/4 inch apart, in the outer edge of the spool. Slip the tag end of the leader through one hole and out the other. You'll find that the

material will never fall off the spool and it's easy to push the line out of the hole when you need another length.

36. CHECK FOR NICKS — Monofilament is drastically weakened if it gets nicks, so it's necessary to check for them. Position the monofilament between the first finger and the thumb. Make sure that the fingernail is firmly

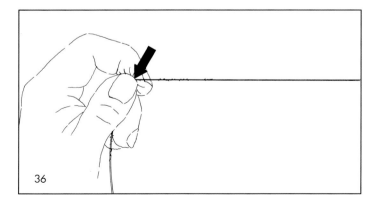

pressed against the monofilament, and then draw the monofilament through the fingers. If there is a nick, the fingernail can detect it easily.

37. LEADER KIT — You can make your own leader kit by purchasing a number of the same sized spools from a manufacturer and then building a plastic box for them as shown in the photo. Before putting the spools in the box, drill small holes in the center of the box opposite where each spool will sit. Then glue a piece of rubber on the *inside* of the box covering the holes.

Put the spools in the box and thread each spool's leader material through the eye of a needle. Force the needle through the rubber and towards the outside of the box. After removing the needle from the monofilament, the leader material will hang outside the box. The rubber prevents it from slipping back inside. Do this for each leader spool and label the leader strengths on the outside of the box for quick reference.

37

38. STORING HEAVY STRAIGHT STRANDS — When removed from storage spools, monofilament that is used for shock leaders, typically in line strengths from 60 to 120 pounds, comes off the spool in small coils. In this form, a shock leader of such heavy monofilament will not impart lifelike action to the fly.

Here are two ways to straighten heavy monofilament. One method is to insert as many strands as possible into a small diameter piece of copper pipe. I use a length of 3/4-inch pipe. Place the pipe in a pan of water, bring the water to a boil, and quickly douse the pipe and strands with cold water, which should straighten all strands. Another method is to suspend the heavy monofilament from a stout weight, and after a time the line will be straight. After you have straightened the strands, clip them to the desired length and store inside a section of one-half inch plastic pipe.

39. FRAYED MONOFILAMENT IS BAD — Many fresh and saltwater species of fish can abrade a leader. After catching any large fish, *always* check a foot or two of your leader

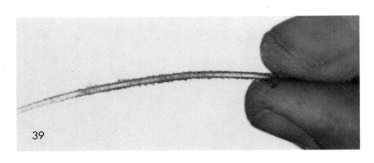

39

directly above the hook. There's a good chance that the leader will need to be clipped and retied.

40. TRIM THOSE LEADER KNOTS — Many anglers will tie a knot in a tapered leader and then carelessly clip off the excess. This leaves small spurs or stubs, which can create problems. For one thing, on the cast the tippet section often travels close to the rest of the leader as it unfolds and moves toward the target. These untrimmed appendages will snag the tippet and spoil the cast. Also, when a hooked fish swims through underwater vegetation, these same stubs or spurs can pick up an amazing amount of grass, adding weight which will cause the tippet to break.

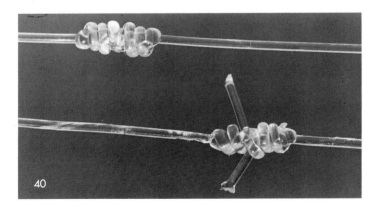

40

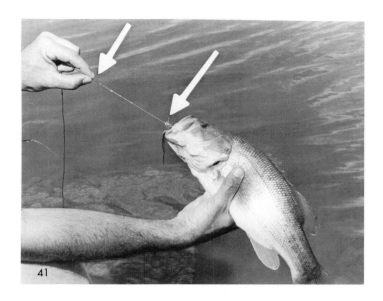

41

41. SHORTEN THE LEADER WITH SINKING LINES —
For many years we fished sinking lines with long leaders
which were developed for floating line applications. But anglers who now routinely fish with sinking fly lines know
that a monofilament leader tends to loft higher than the line
when descending to the fish. Also, they have learned that
shorter leaders will allow you to sink the fly almost as fast
as the line. The photo shows a large mouth bass that took a
fly fished on a seven-inch leader! When fishing a sinking
line, only when waters are extremely clear do you need to
go to longer leaders. You rarely need a leader longer than
three feet with a sinking line.

42. STORING BIMINI TWISTS — Unless you're quite experienced at it, it takes time to build Bimini Twists while on
the water. It's easier to make them at home and have them
available on the boat. Store them together on a spool, loop-

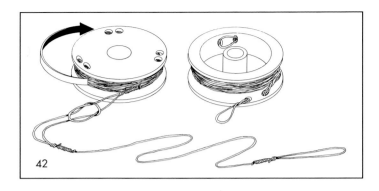

to-loop. Take the spool on the boat with you, and when you need a Bimini Twist, simply un-loop and use it.

43. DON'T THROW AWAY MONOFILAMENT LEADER MATERIAL — When using monofilament, don't throw the wasted strands on the ground. When lying on the ground, monofilament attracts birds since it apparently appears to them to be perfect nesting material. If they pick it up, they may become entangled and consequently suffocate. So either burn your waste monofilament, or bring it home to be properly discarded. (Not illustrated.)

KNOTS

44. METHODS OF ATTACHING LEADERS — Three of the most popular methods of attaching leaders to fly lines are the nail knot, the needle knot, and the loop. There are a lot of books that show you how to tie each one of these. My favorite is the loop, because when properly tied it's stronger than the line, and it allows you to change leaders very quickly and conveniently. Another way of attaching leaders is what I call "the glued connection," in which the leader

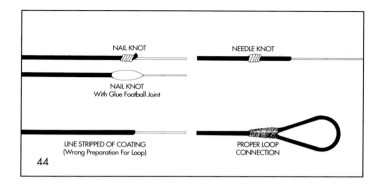

NAIL KNOT

NEEDLE KNOT

NAIL KNOT
With Glue Football Joint

LINE STRIPPED OF COATING
(Wrong Preparation For Loop)

PROPER LOOP
CONNECTION

44

butt is glued inside the front end of the line. But a good glued connection can generally only be constructed properly by a professional. Amateurs usually fail at the job.

At the top left above is the nail knot, and immediately below it, the same knot to which has been added a football joint (discussed in Tip Number 45) so that the nail knot will flow smoothly through the rod guides. At the top right is the needle knot. At the bottom left is shown — for the purpose of emphasizing *how not to prepare* a line before making the loop — the end of a line from which the coating has first been stripped off. Even though many fly fishermen prepare their loops in this manner, it is not the proper way to do it, as loops tied on an uncoated line have a tendency to slip. Instead (as shown at the bottom right) a better way to create a loop knot is to whip the loop right on top of the coated line, so that the whipped thread embeds and secures itself deeply into the line coating, imparting additional strength to the loop.

45. NAIL KNOTS CAN JAM— The most popular method of joining a leader to a fly line is the nail knot. But nail knots can create a lump, or rough joint, which can jam inside the rod guides when a fish near you is trying to escape.

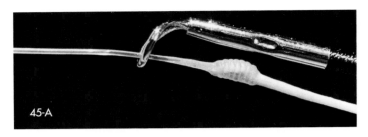

45-A

45-B

To avoid this problem, you need to add a smooth, football-shaped joint to the knot to allow it to pass smoothly through the rod guides. Simply coat the knot with Pliobond, GOOP, or any other flexible glue.

46. TESTING NEW KNOTS — To accurately check any new knot to see if it compares favorably with the one you have been using, take two identically sized hooks. Select a piece of monofilament and tie your old knot to one of the hooks. Tie the new knot to the other hook. Be sure to care-

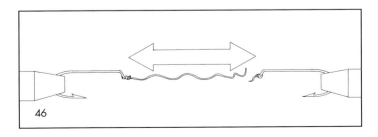

46

fully draw the new knot closed. Then, grasp each hook with a pair of pliers (you'll need a set of pliers for each hook). With steady pressure, pull both hooks apart until one of the knots breaks. Repeat this test at least a dozen times. Then try grasping the hooks with the pliers and jerking the pliers quickly apart. Repeat this at least a dozen times. Many knots that perform well on a slow, steady pull will fail if a sudden jerk occurs, so you need to check the knots both ways before deciding which one is better.

HOOKS

47. TESTING HOOKS FOR SHARPNESS — Aside from the newer chemically or laser-sharpened hooks, you can assume that any new hook, just out of the box, is not sharp enough to use while fishing. Consider the inside of a fish's mouth. It has to be tougher than a bad mother-in-law, since a fish doesn't get to cook or tenderize its meals. So fish are used to grabbing bait that can be very sharp, such as the protruding spines of a minnow or the sharp claws of a crayfish or crab.

47

You will drastically reduce your chances of impaling your hook in your quarry if its point is dull. So it's important to determine if the hook is sharp enough. To do this, press the point of the hook against your thumbnail with a very gentle downward pressure, dragging the point across the nail. If the hook is dull, it will slide along the nail; if sharp enough, it will dig or stick into the nail.

It's a good idea to occasionally check the hook point while you are fishing, since during your back casts you may have damaged it against a rock or stump. Also, anytime you land a fish, check the point before making another cast.

48. FILING DOWN THE BARB — Few people believe my statement (until they have tried it for themselves) that barbless hooks will catch more fish than hooks with large barbs — with the exception only of high-jumping fish, like sailfish and tarpon. It's been my practice for a number of years to use barbless hooks, for a number of reasons: it's kinder to the fish when released; you set the hook better and end up landing more fish; and, if you impale yourself with a hook, it's so much easier to remove. So, you're conserving wildlife as well as your body when you use barbless hooks.

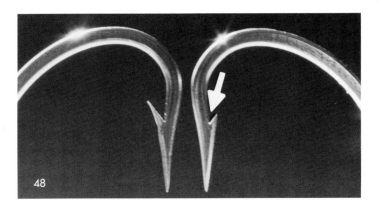

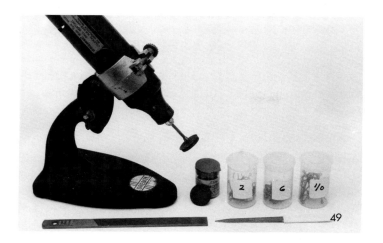

49.

49. HOOK SHARPENING TOOLS — The best file for sharpening larger hooks (sizes 6 to 12/0) is made by Normark, the same company that makes the Rapala fishing lure. This file, costing about five dollars, is the best single file that I have ever used. Another good file is a six-inch Nicholson Smooth, available in some hardware stores.

But there are a number of tools, other than a file, that you can use to sharpen hooks. Take a hobby tool grinder and some round sanding disks, and you have a wonderful tool for sharpening larger hooks. You will need a foot-speed control with this equipment, since the very high speed at which turning grinders operate will heat the hook too much, and as a result, ruin the temper of the hook. By grinding the points slowly, using the foot control, you can quickly produce a perfect diamond point. To further avoid overheating, frequently dip the hook in a cup of water during the grinding process.

For small fresh water hooks, perhaps the best tool is a ladies' fingernail file. Though sometimes called a "diamond dust" file, it is really a layer of silicon carbide mounted on an aluminum paddle. One side has a slightly finer grit than the other. Hooks from size 1 down to about size 10 can be quickly sharpened on the coarser side. Hooks as fine as size 22 can have the points touched up on the smoother side. You can purchase these files at any store where fingernail polish is sold.

Ceramic stones, such as those made by Umpqua Feather Merchants (address: P.O. Box 700, Glide, Oregon 97433) are also good tools. The Umpqua tool has both a rough and smooth side, and is extremely hard. Another asset of this tool is that it doesn't rust. I always carry one in my pocket when I'm fishing.

50. DIAMOND POINT HOOK SHARPENING — Though some anglers prefer using hooks with round points, which are good puncturing tools for fish that have soft mouths, I prefer to use hooks with cutting edges that end at a sharp point. I especially recommend this type of hook point for saltwater fishing, where you will encounter fish with very tough mouths.

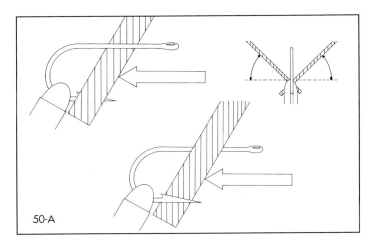

50-A

My favorite hook is one with a diamond point which has four cutting edges that end at a sharp, well-supported point. This point is easy to make with a file. A file is better than a stone, since its flat edges can scrape metal away. (Except for the ceramic type, stones form grooves which prevent the formation of a flat surface on the hook point.)

When you make a diamond point, you are going to end up with a shape (when viewed from the front) that will look like an upside-down/right-side-up pup tent. (I think everyone knows what a pup tent looks like.) First hold the hook so that the barb is facing down and to your right. Place the file on the inside of the barb side, tilting it away from the hook at about a 45-degree angle. Run the file in firm strokes toward the hook bend, creating a 45-degree surface on the hook which will resemble one side of an upside-down pup tent. Now place the file on the outside of the hook point, and run it in firm strokes toward the hook bend, again with the file tilted at about 45 degrees, creating a second 45-degree surface on the hook — the other side of the upside-down pup tent.

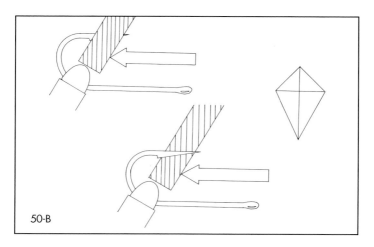

50-B

Now turn the hook so that the barb side is facing up and to your right, and repeat these two filing steps on the opposite, exterior side of the point. After both sides of the hook have been filed in this manner, when it is viewed from the front, you should see a diamond-shaped point with four surfaces, two that look like an upright pup tent on the outside of the bend; and two that look like an upside-down pup tent on the inside of the bend. Note the four cutting edges that are sharp as knives, and which culminate into a well-supported diamond point.

51. USE VISE GRIPS TO HOLD LARGER FLIES WHEN SHARPENING THEM — If you tie your own flies, the best time to sharpen a hook is before you start dressing the hook. If a fly is new and store-bought or has been fished, it will usually need sharpening.

When sharpening a hook, the file should always be stroked from the point toward the rear or bend. If the file is stroked in the other direction, the motion will leave a small, metal burr on the point, even though a sharp point has already been established.

Holding the hook securely is difficult when you have to stroke the hook from the point to the rear. Use the smallest pair of vise grips (a type of pliers available in many hardware stores) for the job. (*Not illustrated.*)

52. HOOK FILE SHEATH — Even though a metal file is the best tool for sharpening larger hooks (sizes 6 through 12/0), it can rust, especially if exposed to saltwater. But there are a few tricks you can use to protect a good file while fishing. Keep the file coated with a light film of WD-40 or a similar protective lubricant. And, for more protection, store the file in a waterproof container. One of the best containers is a 1" or 2" x 7" sheath, made from a plastic envelope. This

52

type of envelope can often be purchased at fly shops or tackle stores. You'll find that bucktail jigs, flies, and other lures are often packaged in them.

To make the sheath, you'll need only scissors or a razor blade and some duct tape. Cut a length of tape slightly longer than the envelope and cover the envelope with it. Fold the excess over the sealed end. Since the tape is narrow, it will only partially cover the envelope, so you'll need to repeat the procedure until the outside is covered completely. Then, cut several one-inch-wide strips and place them at the mouth of the envelope (inside and out) so that you can slip a file in and out easily.

53. LONGER HOOKS MEAN BETTER STRIKES — Many popping bugs are designed with short shank hooks, which puts the point under the body of the bug, thus restricting the effectiveness of hooking the fish. So be sure to use popping bugs that have a point that extends well behind the bug body. Short shanks on bugs tend to cause them to sit flat on the water, which means they don't pop as loudly or pick up as easily with a long line. Longer shank hooks also

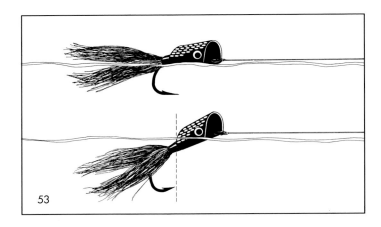

53

cause bugs to tilt (as shown in the illustration), which results in better hook-ups and easier lifts from the surface.

FLIES

54. SEVEN BASIC DRY FLIES FOR TROUT — There are so many dry fly patterns that it must overwhelm a novice angler when he or she walks into a tackle shop. Anglers are constantly wanting to know what flies to use for trout fishing. Fortunately, for most situations there is a simple answer.

First, it is important to recognize that a trout will take caddis flies, terrestrials, and mayflies, all of which produce adult insects that fall to the water. You need to be able to attempt a fair imitation of these. When offering a fly to a trout, you'll need to have duplicated its shape, color, and, most importantly, size, since all insects come in several sizes. Because size is the most important criteria, your dry fly should be fairly close to the size of the flies that trout are feeding on. Next, consider the shape — caddis, terrestrials, and mayflies all differ in this regard. Don't forget about color, though in many cases it doesn't really have a bearing on whether fish take or not.

There are seven flies that will do the job most of the time, but you will have to offer them in different sizes, usually ranging from 12 to 18. Here is the list:

Situation	Type of Fly
Light flies falling into water	Light Cahill
Dark flies falling into water	Adams
Terrestrials	Ant Grasshopper
Caddis flies	Elk Hair Caddis
Rough water, needing a buoyant fly	Royal Wulff Humpy

HUMPY

ADAMS

ANT

LIGHT CAHILL

ROYAL WULFF

ELK HAIR CADDIS

GRASSHOPPER

54

If you'll arm yourself with these seven flies in different sizes and stay observant, you can come to the stream and usually do well. Be sure to notice what kind of insect is floating on the surface and what the trout are taking. So, for example, if a small cream-colored Sulphur fly is hatching, then use a Light Cahill.

One last tip: keep in mind that hoppers don't emerge completely and fall into the stream. They are relatively small in the early part of the season and become larger in the later season. So fish a smaller hopper imitation early and a bigger pattern later.

55. STORE THAT FLY SAFELY — There is a little wire guide, called a ring keeper, located just forward of the handle on almost all fly rods. Almost anyone who has fly fished for a long time has probably stored his fly in this ring keeper and has also probably impaled his hand on the point of the fly when handling the rod. To prevent this from happening again, slip the hook point under the hood at the forward end of the reel seat. This routine will protect your hands and eliminate problems.

56. OILING YOUR DRY FLY — Many trout fishermen dip their dry fly in oil, then after a good dousing, cast it to a fish. The oil will improve the fly's flotation, but if you dip the dry fly in oil and then immediately cast to the fish, you'll often fail to get a fish. This is because any oil that has not been thoroughly dried will form a circular prism around the fly, which will discourage any trout from taking your offering. So after you have dressed a fly, false cast it several times, drop the fly into the water, well away from the fish, and then drag the fly under the surface and false cast again to get it thoroughly dry. This time when you cast the fly, there won't be a telltale prism. (*Not illustrated.*)

57. HANDY CHEST FLY BOX — Because fly boxes come in so many sizes, it's often difficult and even exasperating for fishermen to fit the different sized boxes into the pockets of their fishing vests. Instead, try using a chest box that hangs around the neck. These boxes have multiple compartments that will hold almost all the flies that you might need for a day or even an extended fishing trip, and are easy to carry and work with.

58. USE A FOAM BLOCK — If you wade, you have probably taken a tumble and fallen in the water at one time or another, thoroughly soaking your fly boxes. Unless the contents of the boxes are removed almost immediately and allowed to dry, the hooks will rust and the flies will become damaged.

But you actually only need a few flies when wading. So instead of carrying several boxes with a lot of flies you won't need, use a foam block to carry flies. Insert a string through a block of foam (preferably a closed-cell foam, like Dow Chemical's Ethafoam). Slip the string around your neck and store the necessary flies in this foam block. Another advantage to using the foam block is that it makes it easy to get to the flies when fishing.

58

59-A

59-B

59. GREAT LARGE FLY CARRIER — Many containers have been designed to carry large flies — streamers, bucktails, popping bucks and all the various saltwater patterns — but my favorite is this special soft pack which was originally designed for carrying plastic worms by Bass Pro (address: 1935 South Campbell, Springfield, Missouri 65807).

It's a flat carrier with multiple, see-through pockets, each with its own zipper. It's easy to open, so can you can instantly identify and select your desired pattern. The best part is that it's inexpensive, too.

60. DOPE YOUR FLIES AHEAD OF TIME — Don't waste time on the stream dressing your dry flies so that they will float. Instead, when you finish tying flies, wait until the cement is thoroughly dry, and then apply dry fly oil. The flies are now already treated in advance. (*Not illustrated.*)

61. SOAK THOSE FLOATING FLIES — When you are fishing sinking flies that tend to float, there's a trick to getting them down quickly. Carry a few Ziploc bags with you, and ten minutes or so before you decide to use a wool head,

muddler, sculpin or similar fly, soak it in water that you've enclosed in the Ziploc bag. The wet fly will sink immediately.

62. HAIR DRYERS ARE GREAT — Flies that get mashed out of shape can often be restored quickly and painlessly. The old method of holding a deformed fly over a steam kettle is outdated. It's better to dampen your flies well, then place them in a large tea strainer. Then, cover the open end of the strainer with a piece of cheesecloth, small screen wire, or similar material. Then using the full heat of a hair dryer, blow them dry. The damp flies will be dry in only a short time, and the hackles will be restored to near-perfect condition. (*Not illustrated.*)

63. KEEP SAMPLES — If someone on the stream is really on to the fish with a particular fly pattern, and offers it to you, be sure to ask for two of them. Fish with one and save the other. If the fly is really good and you catch a lot of fish, you'll wear out the first fly. But if you keep the second good one, you'll have something that either you or a fly tyer can duplicate. I store such patterns in a separate, air-tight box, with notes about each fly. Later, I can remove the fly and duplicate it for the right fishing situation. *(Not illustrated.)*

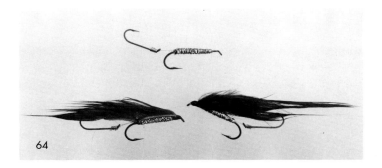

64

64. CATCH THOSE SHORT STRIKERS — Many fish, especially trout, have a tendency to sneak up behind a streamer fly and nip it at the rear, resulting in a missed strike. Snelling a small "stinger" hook on the shank before you start dressing the pattern will eliminate this problem.

65. WIRE WEEDGUARD — While monofilament is the standard material for weedguards, I favor stainless steel trolling wire. This material is tougher and, I feel, makes a better guard. I use a number 5 trolling wire for flies in sizes 6 to 1/0, and a number 7 for larger flies. The illustration shows how to install a weedguard. Attach the wire in the

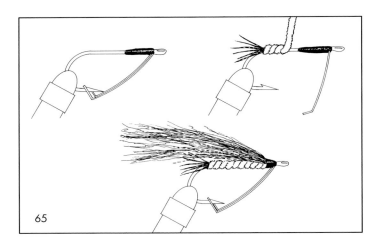

65

form of a shallow horseshoe, making sure that the bend is just forward of the barb. Bend the guard straight down from the hook shank and tie the fly. Then, lodge the guard on the hook in front of the barb, just back of the point.

66. SINGLE WEEDGUARD — You can make a simple weedguard for any popping bug that you already have in your inventory. Take a needle and insert it at an angle into the bug body. For this procedure, use a sharp pointed stub

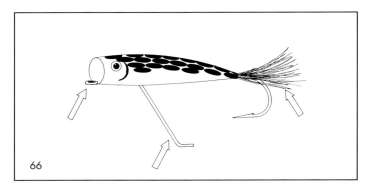

66

of monofilament, preferably about the size of the hook diameter or even a bit larger. When you withdraw the needle, insert the sharpened end of the monofilament into the hole. Place one drop of fast-setting glue over the point of penetration. The end of the monofilament should be slightly lower than the hook point, and can be bent, as shown, with a pair of pliers.

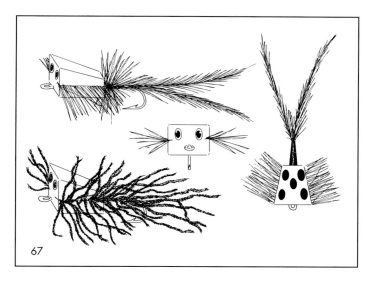

67. A BETTER GERBUBBLE BUG — The Gerbubble Bug is one of the best largemouth bass popping bugs. It is usually dressed with chicken neck feathers, but try using marabou feathers instead, since when a bug dressed in this manner is twitched by the angler and allowed to sit still, the softer marabou feathers will continue to undulate for a much longer time than chicken feathers. Starting at the upper left and proceeding clockwise, this illustration shows side, front and top views of the standard chicken feather tie, and at the lower left, the bug tied with marabou feathers.

68. COIN TUBES ARE HANDY — Sharpen hooks and crush the barbs before you actually tie a fly. When I have a few spare moments, I do this. Doing it beforehand is easier, since sometimes points will break when you press down the barb on a highly tempered hook. So, doing it before you take the trouble to tie the fly is easier.

I keep the treated hooks in small coin storage tubes, properly labeled. These tubes can be purchased in hobby shops or where old coins are sold. (*Not illustrated.*)

69. HANDY STORAGE AREA — When tying flies, I used to have a hard time finding certain materials. So I bought one of these multi-drawer storage cabinets that has anywhere from 20 to 40 small drawers. They are available in most hardware stores. Now I can keep things like spare bobbins, small tying tools, whip finishers, scissors, etc., close to the desk and always within easy reach. I find the cabinet is also the best place for storing hooks of size 6 and larger that I use for bass and saltwater flies. Additionally, because the drawers are labeled, I find what I need quickly, so tying is more fun and productive.

70.

70. VISE BACKGROUND — Nothing in the house is usually in more disarray than a fly tying table. When most of us tie, it's difficult to see the fly against a messy or cluttered background. A good way to eliminate this problem is to position a small piece of light-colored cardboard behind the vise, so that when you're tying, the brightly colored fly is positioned against this neutral background. I prefer using a very light green background, since it seems the most relaxing color on my eyes.

71. TUBING GRIPS — If your hackle pliers constantly slip when gripping a feather, there is an easy way to make them grasp better and not cut the feather. Purchase some soft plastic or rubber tubing in a small diameter from your local druggist. You don't need to buy a lot; an inch of it is enough to do several hackle pliers. Clip off about 1/4 inch and slip it *on only one of the jaws*. It works great! (*Not illustrated.*)

72. SAND AWAY SPURS — When tying flies, many people, especially those who work outdoors and have rough hands, will find that tiny spurs of skin will catch in the finer threads or make it very difficult to work with dubbing. To remove these spurs and make the skin smooth, rub a Dr. Scholl's Skin Dressing Stone (available in most drug stores) over the roughened skin area. Two or three swipes is usually all that will be needed. (*Not illustrated.*)

73. CAPTURE CEMENTS — I guess every fly tyer has at one time or another spilled a bottle of cement on the table. If you'll keep your bottles in a foam block, you'll never spill another drop. Cut a block of plastic foam and make holes in it. Size the holes so that your bottles will fit securely in the foam. I also keep bodkin needles in the same block.

73

74

74. CLEARING THE EYES — If there is even a hint of ce-ment in the hook eye of the fly, it's much easier to get rid of it as you are finishing off the fly while the cement is still wet, rather than waiting until later after the cement has hardened. Strip the fluff from the base of a feather, then in-sert the quill into the hook eye and draw the feather through the eye. If the cement is still soft, the feather will clear any excess from the eye.

75. PAINTED FLY EYES — I am convinced that streamers with large eyes will draw more strikes when you're fishing in clear water. There are many kinds of eyes that can be used for flies: various sizes of bead chain; lead eyes; Mylar eyes; or painted feathers.

Let's look first at painting large eyes on feathers, which is a good technique if you do not want to add appreciable weight to the streamer pattern. Take several breast feathers from a goose or duck. Strip the fuzz from the base of the feather and support the feather with a clothespin, so that it sits upright. I generally do this with a dozen or more feathers at a time.

Now, coat the feathers with a clear-head, vinyl, or similar cement. Then, using round wooden pegs dipped in hobby paint (I like enamel), place a large dot on the feather. After the first dot of paint is dry, position a smaller one in the center of the first dot. When dry, these feathers can be tied on any new or existing streamer. Before tying the feather to the fly, it should be trimmed to a size that is equal to the fly. (*Not illustrated.*)

76. LEAD EYES — If you want more weight on your streamer to help sink the fly deeper into the water column, lead eyes that you can paint directly on the finished head of the fly will serve fine as an optic to attract fish.

76

Lefty fishing with a six-foot square of 1/4" mesh to cover the "line catchers" in his boat. See Tip Number 102. ➤

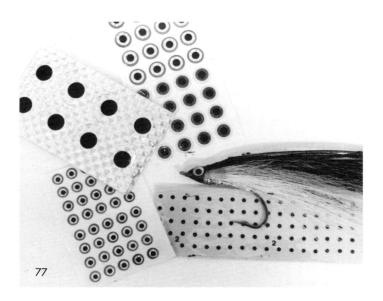

77

77. MYLAR EYES — My favorite method for adding eyes to a streamer without increasing its weight is to use those made of Mylar. These eyes have a glue on the back which holds them lightly in position on the fly. You then have to secure them with a coating of epoxy or several coats of clear-head cement. Mylar eyes come in many sizes and colors. They are available at most fly shops.

78. TRIMMING BUCKTAIL — There is a neat trick that I stumbled onto many years ago while fly tying which, I feel, makes it easier to work with bucktail as well as to obtain more material from each tail. If you turn a bucktail over with the skin side facing up, you'll see a long dark "V" in the center of the hide, which then tapers off toward the tail. This "V" is actually the darker part of the hair.

Using a scalpel or razor blade, slice along each side of the dark "V", separating the bucktail into three pieces (two out-

78

side pieces and the center). Carefully trim away the dark hairs on the two outer pieces and the light hairs from the center piece. You should have two outer edges and a center piece of a pure color. Now you can clip the desired color from the bucktail more quickly without wasting any material. Also, these pieces are easier to store when not in use.

79. CUTTING ZONKER STRIPS — The zonker, made with a wing of a narrow strip of rabbit, is a super streamer pattern. It's easiest to buy pre-cut Zonker strips, but if you want to cut them from a hide yourself, note that you can't cut the hide right on a table. If you do, you'll slice the hair on the other side that is mashed against the table. So, you'll need to have the rabbit hide supported well, with nothing behind it, in order to cut strips.

With a large spring clamp, firmly secure the hide on one side to the table. Stretch the hide across the table and apply

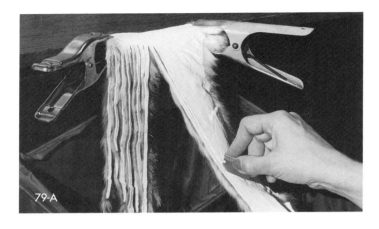

79-A

another clamp at the other side. The hide is now taut. Now hold the bottom of the hide and cut as many strips as desired with a single-edged razor blade.

Or a better way to do this is to secure several razor blades with two very small screws. Each blade should be separated with washers, depending on the desired strip widths. With this rig you can make one swipe and cut several strips exactly the width of the separated blades.

79-B

80. BEAD CHAIN WORKS — Try using a bead chain instead of wire to hang your flies. The flies will stay between the beads and never move.

81. BUG CLIPS — Painted popping bugs are the very devil to hold in position while the paint dries on them. But you can make dandy holders for just a few dollars. Purchase any number of alligator clips from a local electrical store. Drive

some nails through a small board and glue the clips to the nails. Now you can use the clips to hold the bugs in position while they dry.

82

82. ANGLE THE STREAMERS — When you coat the head of a streamer with clear cement and then stick the fly in a block of foam, most of the cement tends to sag to the underside of the head. To prevent this, coat the head and immediately impale the fly in a foam block so that the fly is pointed nearly vertically. Any excess cement will flow down evenly around the head and into the base of the feathers or hair forming the wing. This trick will eliminate that saggy lump on the bottom of the fly head and in addition provide a wing that is better sealed.

83. DRUMS ARE FOR DRYING — If you get into tying many flies where you are using five or 10-minute epoxy, you know that one of the most bothersome tasks is trying to keep the soft glue from sagging out of shape until the epoxy hardens. Obtain a rotisserie motor, or a special motor

used for drying the finish coating on rods (available at Dale Clemens Custom Tackle, 444 Schantz Spring Road, Allentown, Pennsylvania 18104, or any other rod component supplier). Attach a round foam block to the motor. Apply a coating of epoxy to the fly and quickly insert the hook into the round foam block. Turn the motor on and the block will rotate, evenly spreading the epoxy on the fly while it sets. You can add more flies as the wheel turns.

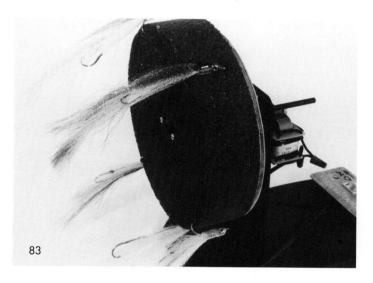

83

84. CUTTING LATEX — You can make beautifully serrated bodies for nymphs using latex rubber. You'll need narrow and sometimes varying widths of latex for the purpose. Latex rubber is thin and difficult to cut, so place a piece of masking tape on one side of the latex while cutting. You can cut any desired shape this way. (*Not illustrated.*)

OVERLEAF: *Fishing boats on Lake McDonald, Glacier National Park, Montana. See Tips Number 102-109 for Lefty's boat tips.*

CHAPTER TWO

EQUIPMENT TIPS

BOOTS, WADERS, AND WADING STAFFS

85. CHECKING FOR HOLES— If your boots or waders leak, there is a quick way to locate the problem holes. Go into a dark room and insert a lighted flashlight inside the boot. Move it around while you look at the outside of the boot. If there are any holes, pinpoints of light will show. *(Not illustrated.)*

86. SOAKING UP YOUR BOOTS — There are many waterproofing pastes that you can put on boots to keep water out. The problem with most of these pastes is that they merely remain on the outer skin and never become fully absorbed throughout the leather, which is the key to waterproofing.

To overcome this problem, thoroughly coat the boots with the paste, sit them on a piece of aluminum foil or something to catch waste, and then, using a hair dryer on its warmest setting, heat the paste until it seeps well into the leather and is fully absorbed. Wipe off any excess and your well-treated boots are ready. *(Not illustrated)*.

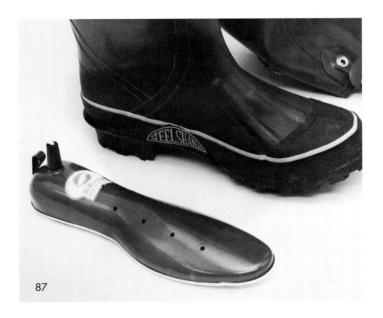

87

87. HEATED BOOT DRYERS — When you get boots wet, or even damp, a pair of electrical boot dryers is a lifesaver. These are tiny metal heaters shaped like slippers. They get warm, never hot, and won't harm boots. And they'll dry most boots overnight. Just stick a metal slipper in each boot and plug into an electrical outlet.

88. COFFEE CANS AND PLASTIC PIPE — Most anglers hang boots upside down to dry them, which limits the amount of circulation and slows the drying process. A better method is to have the boots stand upright, while insuring that they remain open.

But it's difficult to keep boots open, so I found a great device to do the job. Simply remove the top and bottom from a one-pound coffee can and position it inside the boot, so that it holds the boot open (you might need two cans).

You can flatten the cans to carry them in your baggage for use on a trip.

With waders, coffee cans are not long enough to hold them open properly. So substitute a short section of three-inch plastic pipe. Use about 20 to 24 inches of pipe for each leg. The pipe is then long enough to hold the waders open while they dry.

89. BOOTS BY THE FURNACE ARE A NO-NO — It is a common practice to hang boots or waders beside a hot furnace. But if the boots or waders are made of rubber, then you may shorten their useful life considerably, as the high amount of ozone that is generally emitted by a furnace attacks rubber. If there is any doubt about your furnace, store your boots well away from it. Additionally, be sure to keep them out of direct sunlight. (*Not illustrated.*)

90. HIP BOOT HARNESS — Just about everyone supports their hip boots by a strap which is designed to be affixed to the belt. But some men and women don't wear pants with a belt, so instead they have to hang their hip boots on their pants, causing their pants to sag under the strain of supporting the added weight of the hip boots.

I recommend using a boot harness. You may want to purchase one. They are hard to find, but some catalogs still carry them. Or you can make your own by using a wide piece of strapping and two "D" rings, available from many marine store outlets. The harness hangs over the shoulders and the boot straps go through the "D" rings. This way the boots are supported by the shoulders, not your pants.

91. VACUUM THOSE BOOTS — A vacuum cleaner can dry boots quickly, but it should always be on a cool setting. A hot setting will destroy the rubber in most boots. (*Not illustrated.*)

92. DON'T FOLD WADERS — Perhaps the best method to store waders is to have them hang upright. But if it's not convenient for you to hang them, don't fold them. Simply roll them up for storage. This will prevent the formation of sharp folds or wrinkles, which will in time cause waders to crack. (*Not illustrated.*)

93. BOOT STRAP SNAGS — One of the most bothersome things about wearing hip boots is that the fly line constantly snags in the dangling strap, as shown below.

93-A

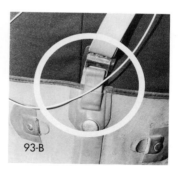
93-B

It's easy to solve this problem. Simply remove the strap from its buckle, reverse the buckle's position, and insert the strap. Now the strap will go inside the boot and won't get tangled in the line.

94

94. CHEST HIGH WADERS — I recommend using chest high waders in cold water situations, such as cold spells in Florida's Everglades (as shown here) or in the freezing waters of Alaska. Neoprene waders are much warmer than the lighter cloth types. They normally are manufactured in two thicknesses, three mm. and five mm., the latter being the one to use if you do a lot of cold water wading.

95. SAVE YOUR SOLES — Felt-soled boots and waders are often necessary if you want to stay upright in many waters. But since felt is relatively soft, it will wear out and eventually need to be replaced. For many years I replaced the soles myself, sometimes requiring a lot more time than I wanted to spend on it.

Finally, it dawned on me that the local shoe repairman could do the job for just a few dollars. Now I buy the felt soles and let the repairman do the rest. (*Not illustrated.*)

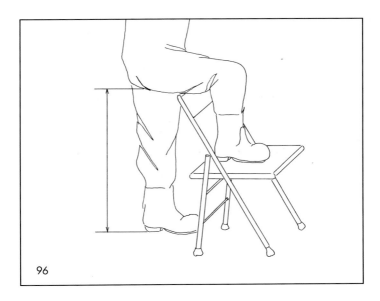

96

96. GET THE CORRECT LENGTH WADERS — The
illustration shows an easy way to make sure that your
waders fit properly, so far as leg length is concerned. Slip a
test pair on and place your leg over a chair. If you can't
accomplish this maneuver easily, then you need to continue
trying other pairs until you can.

97. ATTACHING CORD TO WADING STAFF — Since
most wading staffs are equipped with a short length of rope
or flexible bungee cord attached to the staff below the
handle, when fly line is retrieved and dropped into the
water beside the angler, it frequently becomes entangled in
the handle of the wading staff that is protruding above the
attached cord.

You can eliminate this problem by re-attaching the cord
in a new location, at the top of the handle. Drill a hole in
the top end of the staff and glue the cord or rope into the

.97

opening. Now the rod handle will not get in the way and your line can slide freely on the water.

98. WADING STAFF CORDS — Now attach the other end of the cord to one of the "D" rings of your wading vest.

When not using the staff, raise it over your head and drop it over your back, as shown.

Now with the staff nestled between the shoulder blades, your hands remain free, and the staff won't drag on the ground while walking. When needed, slide the cord off the shoulder by leaning your body to the side.

98-A

98-B

98-C

99. PACKAGE YOUR CLOTHES FOR WET TRIPS — If there is a remote chance that your luggage might get wet on a trip, you need to take precautions. Salt spray from a running boat, rain, or a dunking in a river, can get clothing so wet that it may not be dry for days. Whenever I feel that my clothing or any other items I want to keep dry may be exposed to the elements, I package them in plastic bags. Use the plastic your daily newspaper arrives in. Using this trick, on several occasions I have been the only angler in camp with dry clothes.

100. PUT YOUR ADDRESS ON THE BAG — If you use a duffle bag when you travel, you should write your name on the outside of the bag with a permanent marking pen. Lug-

gage tags can be lost, making it difficult for the airlines to track your bag. But never put your telephone number on the outside of the bag, for then if it is stolen, the thieves can't call your number and find out that no one is home.

For anyone who uses hard luggage, take two extra precautions: tape your home address on the *inside* of your luggage; and also tape a note inside with the specifics of your travel plans. If your bag is misdirected and the luggage tag is lost, when the airlines locate and open the bag, they can determine whether to send the luggage to your vacation destination or to your home. *(Not illustrated.)*

101. SOFTEN DUFFLE BAGS — Use soft duffle bags when traveling to remote fishing areas. As you pack, if you will add two or three layers of bubble pack on both the top and bottom of the bag, you will make a very neat cushion that will soften any impact the bag may receive in transit. Additionally, the plastic foam will also help keep the top and bottom dry, in case it rains or the bag is placed on wet ground. *(Not illustrated.)*

BOATS, ANCHORS, AND TRAILERS

102. NET YOUR BOAT — When you're fishing from boats, there are all sorts of things that can get caught on the fishing line. But you can use nets to eliminate the problem. Buy about six square feet of netting, available from commercial fish houses. (You can also order it from the Netcraft Company, 2800 Tremainsville Road, Toledo, Ohio 43613.) Place several 1/8 or 1/4-inch, pinch-on sinkers around the rim to weigh it down. Now whenever you are fishing from a boat you can throw the net over any objects that may possibly catch your fishing line.

103. MASK THOSE LINE CATCHERS — Use one or two-inch wide masking tape and stretch it across cleats, nails, and any other appendages on the boat that may possibly catch your fly line. The tape can be easily removed at day's end and won't harm the finish on the boat.

104. RAIN-FREE — If you operate a fast-running bonefish skiff, bass boat, or other water craft, you know that without a windshield, driving rain can mar vision and be downright uncomfortable. No problem. Just purchase a motorcycle helmet and wear it when running in the rain.

105. MOTOR FORK — If you operate a boat with a small motor (up to about 25 horsepower) in rocky rivers, as I do, you need to protect your propeller. If you will attach a dung fork, which has four tines, to the lower unit, as shown in the illustration, you can eliminate the problem.

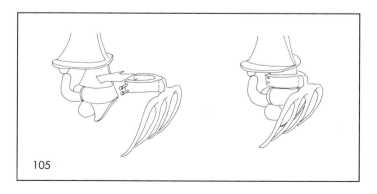

105

106. STOP THAT MOANING — When hauling something on the roof of our cars, many of us have heard that loud moaning sound that is caused by the vibration of air as it passes over the cargo strapping. This objectionable noise is easy to eliminate. Simply place one or two twists in the strap. It will get rid of the noise and also save wear and tear on the strapping.

107. FOAM BLOCKS — For those of you that use foam blocks when carrying boats and canoes on top of the car, here are two tips that will ease this kind of transport. One

suggestion is that you mark your boat with tape or pen at exactly the spot where the blocks should go when positioned properly. In this way, you won't hurt the car's finish by continually dragging the boat back and forth to find the right position for the foam blocks. The other suggestion is to always tighten down the rear of the boat before you tighten the front so that the blocks are firmly held in place, at the rear. If you secure the craft the other way, you take a chance that the rear blocks will not be tight enough, which could spell disaster on the drive home.

108. SPONGE IT AWAY — Nothing beats a sponge for sopping up water in a boat. It's unbreakable, light, soaks up the water, and can also be used to scrub the deck clean. *(Not illustrated.)*

109. CANOE ROD HOLDERS — Nothing is worse for getting in the way inside a canoe than a fly rod. But, you can make simple rod holders to store four rods in a canoe with a small amount of time and money. Follow the illustrations to construct and install such holders.

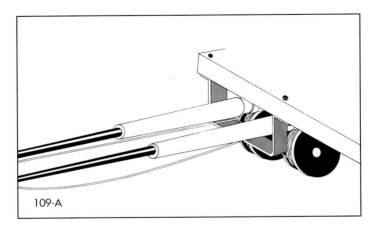

109-A

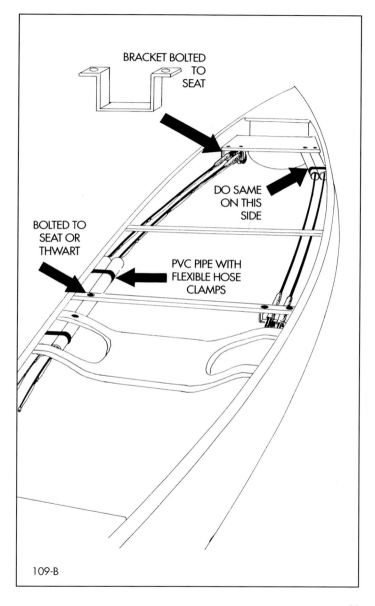

BRACKET BOLTED
TO
SEAT

DO SAME
ON THIS
SIDE

BOLTED TO
SEAT OR
THWART

PVC PIPE WITH
FLEXIBLE HOSE
CLAMPS

109-B

110. DRAG ANCHOR — Whenever you are drifting on a lake or river, and want the boat to travel front first with the current or wind, use a drift anchor, which is a piece of chain attached to a rope. The chain can drag along the bottom, and in deeper lakes, be suspended below the boat in the water column. The resistance it creates tends to make the canoe or boat drift naturally instead of spinning around. If the river has many small rocks that you believe may snag the links in the chain (although this is a rare occurrence), simply enclose the chain within a piece of flexible plastic tubing. Remember, the farther the chain is behind the boat, the more drag it creates.

111. RELEASE ANCHOR — While you're anchored, if you hook a big fish and want to be prepared to follow it quickly while not losing your boat position on the river, use a release anchor. This will allow you to keep the anchor in place while going after that fish.

To make a release anchor, take a crab pot float or any type of small buoy and run a short length of rope through it. Secure it to the bow eye of the boat and attach the an-

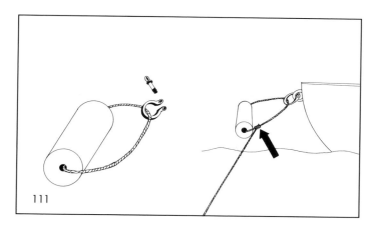

chor line to this. When you have to follow a fish, disconnect the buoy rope from the bow eye, and then chase the fish. When you return, the buoy will be holding your anchor line on the surface, and you can reconnect your float and anchor to the bow eye.

112. ANCHOR CANOE FROM THE REAR — People have lost gear and even drowned by tying the anchor rope to the

side of a canoe. In this position, when the anchor catches on the bottom, the pull of the weight is at the side, which will often cause the canoe to flip over. Use a device that lets you suspend the anchor at the very end of the canoe, so that when anchored there will be a safer pull on the craft. Additionally, keeping the anchor suspended on the outside of the boat will prevent the mud and dirty water that is usually clinging to it from getting inside the boat.

113

113. MAKING A CANOE ANCHOR — One of the best anchors for a canoe can be made from a pet food can. Place a 1/4-inch steel rod inside the can, with the bent portion rising several inches out of the can. With a gas torch, heat some lead in a camp stove and fill the can with the lead. When filled with lead, the pet food can will weigh six or seven pounds, which should be more than adequate for anchoring a canoe or belly boat.

114. CHECKING TRAILER TIRES — Many fishermen use a boat or camper trailer to haul a craft to the water. Since most trailers have tires that are smaller in diameter than the ones on a car, they rotate at a much higher speed, generating greater heat than the car tires. In addition, if trailer tires are not properly inflated, the resulting reduction in air pressure causes the tires to flex too much, building up even more heat, which will soon ruin the tires.

There are two ways to avoid problems with your trailer tires. First, measure the pressure in your trailer tires before you move it, while the tires are cold, and note how many pounds of air the tires are carrying. For sake of example, let's assume that you get a reading that is five pounds less than the tire manufacturer's recommended pressure. Then after driving a bit, measure the tire again at a gas station. This second pressure reading will often be different than the first one, but no matter what this second reading is, add that five-pound deficit that was determined by your first reading. Second, if you are using tubeless tires, equip them with tubes. This will virtually eliminate tire problems. (*Not illustrated.*)

115. DO IT BACKWARDS — It's difficult backing a trailer, since the steering wheel must be moved in the opposite direction from which the trailer will move. Try positioning

your hand on the bottom of the wheel, rather than in the normal way, on the top. With your hand in this position, if you want the trailer to go left, then simply move your hand in that direction.

116. "X" THOSE CHAINS — When you hook the trailer tongue to the ball hitch on your car, be sure to position the safety chains in an "X" configuration. In that way, should the tongue jump loose, it will fall into the cradle formed by the "X" of chain and the tongue won't drag on the ground.

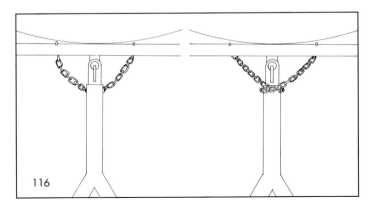

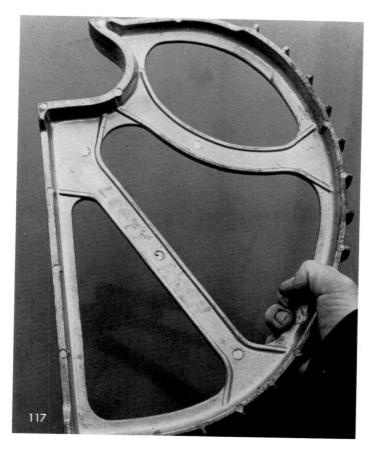

117

117. EASY LIFT TRAILER JACK — If you have ever tried to lift a trailer with a jack to change a tire, you know that you need a very special low jack to get underneath the trailer axle. And because the jack is so low to the ground, it can also be difficult to turn the handle or pump the jack. There is a neat jack (pictured here) which is shaped somewhat like a half moon, with a groove in one side. To elevate the trailer axle, slide this jack under the axle (it's best to

position a board under it so it won't sink into soft ground) and simply move the car, causing the half moon to roll upward, thus lifting the trailer.

118. SECURE BOTH ENDS — If you ever are faced with a stiff cross wind when winding a boat up on your trailer, there is an easy way to control the boat during the operation. Attach a rope at least one and one-half times the boat's length to the windward side, at both the bow and stern. Now you can manipulate the rope to keep the rear of the craft from yawing in the breeze as the boat is brought up on the trailer.

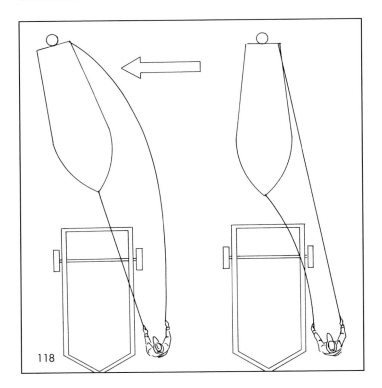

118

MEDICATIONS AND LOTIONS

119. SUNSCREEN AND LIP PROTECTION — It is generally known that sunscreen with at least a SPF number of 15 must be used to prevent too much exposure to the sun. This is especially true for fly fishermen who spend long hours exposed to the sun.

I advise using a *waterproof* sunscreen so that it will remain effective despite heavy perspiration. And to make the sunscreen even more effective, I recommend applying it while still at home or in the hotel room, before you begin to perspire. Give it a full five minutes or more to thoroughly dry. Then apply a second coat. The second coating seems to give longer protection. To prevent developing sun blisters on my lips, I also use lipstick or chapstick that contains aloe. Aloe is a medicinal plant that has the ability to penetrate the skin. It's even better if you can obtain a lotion that contains both aloe and a sunscreen in it. Apply it whenever your lips feel dry. *(Not illustrated.)*

120. BAND-AIDS IN WALLET — I carry two Band-Aids in my wallet — they take up so little room. I find that at least several times a year I will use them, for myself or a fishing buddy. *(Not illustrated.)*

121. DOUBLE YOUR INSECT REPELLENT'S EFFECTIVENESS — If you add a little petroleum jelly (Vaseline or a similar brand) to your non-aerosol liquid insect repellent, you'll find that it seems to last much longer when on the skin. Add just enough of it so that the liquid will still flow freely. *(Not illustrated.)*

122. USE THE BACK OF YOUR HANDS — Many insect repellents are destructive to fly lines, so to prevent getting

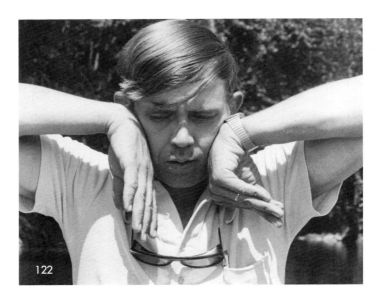

122

the repellent on the inside of your hands and fingers that will have to come in contact with the fly line, put the repellent on the backs of your hands. Then use the backs of your hands to apply the repellent to other parts of your body.

MISCELLANEOUS

123. COPY YOUR PASSPORT AND CARRY PROOFS OF PURCHASE — There are always special problems associated with international travel, but two of the most serious can be avoided by the careful traveler.

As you probably know, passports get stolen all the time when people travel abroad. In fact, on a trip to a foreign country I once took with two other outdoor writers, we all had our passports stolen. But because I had photocopies of mine, I was able to depart the country the same evening.

The other two fellows were stuck there for three extra days.

I suggest you always keep photocopies of your passport. You need only copy the pages that have all the essential data — your photograph, name and address, place and date issued, and most importantly, the passport number.

Don't carry the copies with your passport, because if it is stolen all is lost. Instead, keep the copies scattered in various places (your fishing vest, inside your wallet, etc.) so that you always have one with you. For example, once I was stopped on the Rio Colorado River by soldiers from Nicaragua. I happened to be carrying a copy of my passport in my camera case, and they quickly let me go.

The other travel lifesaver concerns your camera equipment. Contrary to what many people believe, custom agents are pretty nice people — they're simply trying to catch crooks. But if you're returning home with some fine camera equipment, they'll generally require proof that you purchased it in the U. S. Without proof, you may have to pay a substantial duty on the gear.

An easy way to accomplish this is to take your camera equipment to any international airport in your area that has a customs office. You will have to show the equipment to the agent. To save time, make sure you have already copied down all the serial numbers for the bodies and lenses.

They will furnish you with a small form on which to list all your gear. Carry photocopies (the originals are small and easy to lose) of this form with you whenever you travel abroad. I usually carry a copy in my camera case. (*Not illustrated.*)

124. KEEPING NAPKINS DRY — Most experienced anglers know that wearing Polaroid sunglasses will help them see fish better. The glare-removing properties not only allow the angler to peer better into the water, but also relieve eye strain.

But to see well, you need clean glasses, the cleaner the better. Rain, salt spray and other elements will dirty the glasses so that they may need cleaning several times a day. But carrying a handkerchief in your pocket isn't the answer. If the climate is warm, the handkerchief gets damp with perspiration, making it difficult to clean the glasses properly. Instead, take dry paper napkins and place in a plastic bag so they'll stay dry and clean. (*Not illustrated.*)

125. RAIN-X IS GREAT — I discovered this great material called Rain-X, sold at auto stores. When applied to a clean windshield, small raindrops just slip off, even without the wipers running. I don't know what's in this stuff, but it sure gets rid of water on glass.

I got the idea of applying it to the surfaces of my Polaroid non-plastic sunglasses, and discovered that any water that fell on them seemed to slip away instantly.

The trick to properly using Rain-X is to clean the glass surface well before application. Then, simply moisten a rag with it and wipe on the glasses. One application will last for several days. An added plus is that the stuff's inexpensive.

125

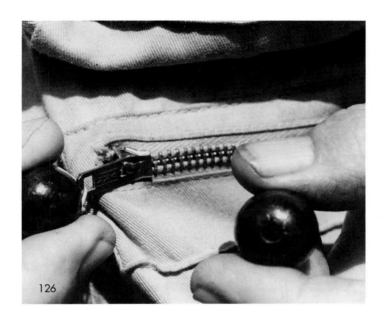

126

126. WOODEN BALLS AND SHOESTRINGS — The tabs on most zippers are too small for most of us, so trying to zip up a rain jacket quickly as a storm approaches is sometimes frustrating. On an over-stuffed fly vest, the tabs are so small you can't even locate them.

I find that attaching a short length of shoestring with a one-inch wooden ball to the tab will solve the problem. Such wooden balls are available at most hardware stores.

127. AN UNBREAKABLE CONTAINER — When carrying soft tubes of glue, sunscreen, or similar travel aids in your luggage, be sure to pack them in something that will prevent their being crushed. You might use a length of plastic pipe to carry all the tubes. Buy two plastic pipe caps as well, so you can use them as lids for both ends of the pipe. The caps will fit snugly if you push them into position. The case

127

is also watertight, so it can be used to store passports and other valuables while fishing aboard an open boat.

128. USE YOUR METAL SCRIBE — Small metal scribing tools, available from many hobby shops and hardware stores, are a great device to employ to put your identification on fishing equipment. The tool's rapidly vibrating, sharp point allows you to write on metal.

128

129. USE THE CORRECT MARKER — Never mark on a map or chart with a pen, because the ink will run if the chart gets wet. Instead use a plain graphite pencil.

130. REVERSE THOSE BATTERIES TO SAVE A LIFE — If the switch on a flashlight, electric razor, or electronic flash is inadvertently turned on for a long period of time, the batteries will soon die. So for many years I have been stor-

ing one of the batteries in the *wrong* position. In that way, if the switch gets turned on accidentally, the conductors will not be touching. Then when needed, I simply put the batteries back into their proper operating positions.

131. MAKE THEM ALL THE SAME — Stranded on a reef in British Honduras many years ago, I struggled for hours to repair the outboard motor of the fishing boat. I nearly made it before the batteries on my flashlight died. Looking around, I realized that I had sixteen AA size batteries for my camera equipment, but not one size of the batteries needed to operate the essential flashlight. So, we sat all night in the dark, waiting for help.

From that day on, I was determined that my travel alarm clock, flashlight, cameras, electronic flash, razor and any other battery-driven units would *all* work on the same size batteries. Experience has proven this was a wise choice.

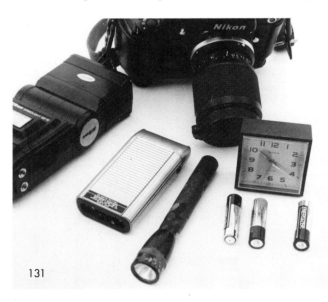

131

132

132. SAFETY WITH A SAFETY PIN — All too frequently when attempting to tie on a fly, you find that the hook eye is sealed with glue. You can usually just insert another hook into the eye of the fly to remove the glue, but this dulls its point. Instead, carry the smallest safety pin that you can buy and attach it to your fishing vest. It will work even on a size 22 hook.

133. STRING UP YOUR PLIERS — Many fly fishermen, especially those that fish in saltwater, carry a pair of fishing pliers. Usually the pliers are carried in a holster supported by the belt. But digging the pliers out of the holster can be bothersome. Since most pliers have a hole in each handle, you can tie a stout piece of string (I use old fly line) between the pliers. Now you have something that you can slip your fingers under, and the pliers can be easily lifted from the holster. Using pop rivets, you can also affix a small piece of sheet aluminum to the holster for storing a ceramic sharpening stone, thus having two tools handy.

Another good point about the string is that it can be tucked under the first finger while working with the pliers.

In a heavy surf or a rocking boat, if the pliers possibly slip out of your hand, they will not be lost, but will remain captured by the string under your small finger.

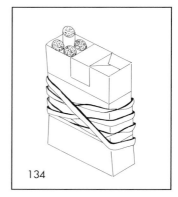

134. DON'T DROP THAT PACK — For a cigarette smoker, nothing can spoil a trip quicker than dropping his butts overboard. So wrap a rubber band around them. The rubber will bind against the inside of the shirt pocket and the pack won't fall out.

135. THE POSITION IS THE THING — When using a tube of glue, never make the mistake of opening the tube,

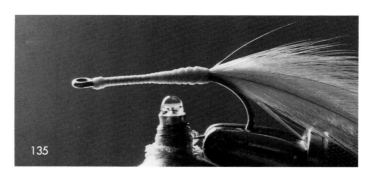

then tilting the tube downward as you force glue from it. This action often causes the glue to spill out entirely too much. Instead, hold the glue upright, with the opening at the top, and slowly squeeze the tube. All the air will be vented and the glue will come out smoothly.

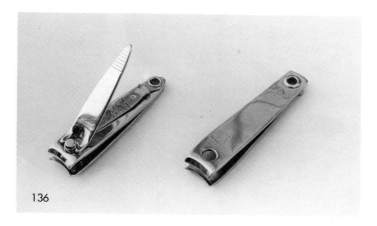

136

136. AN INEXPENSIVE TROUBLE-FREE CLIPPER — Remove the handle from a fingernail clipper and attach it with a short length of string to your fly vest. This modified clipper will now slide easily in and out of your pocket. When cutting leader material, be sure to position the thumb and forefinger directly over the blades as you press them together.

137. NON-SLIP SUNGLASSES — When fishing in hot weather, one of the most bothersome of all problems is sunglasses constantly slipping down on the nose. You push them up and moments later, they are sliding down again. You can solve this problem by attaching a short piece of line (I use old fly line) to each side of the frames. Sew a short length of Velcro to each of the other ends of the strings.

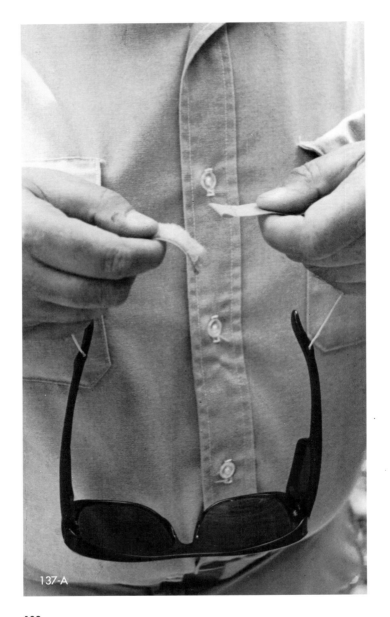

137-A

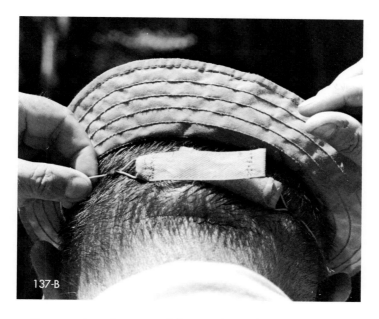

137-B

Put on the glasses and fasten the Velcro strips behind your head to hold the glasses firmly on your nose in the position you find most comfortable. Now they will not move.

Another advantage of this rig is that during hot weather, you can position the glasses a little farther down on the nose to prevent fogging of the lens.

OVERLEAF: *Lefty's recommended "prayer attitude" has paid off for this angler on California's Hat Creek, despite his brightly colored jacket which Lefty does not recommend.*

CHAPTER THREE

TECHNIQUE AND TACTICS TIPS

LOCATING AND APPROACHING FISH

138. USE BINOCULARS TO LOCATE FISH — Binoculars are a great tool, especially when trout fishing. I have found that the best type are four-power models, which are small enough to fit in the pocket of your shirt or fishing vest. Try using them to look over a stream from a distance before you get close to it. It's surprising how many fish you'll locate that you wouldn't see if you had just walked up to the stream bank. You can also frequently see what the trout are feeding on, without going to the trouble of sampling the stream. Maybe the best reason for using binoculars is when a nearby angler is catching fish and you want to know what kind of fly he's using! (Not illustrated.)

139. WEARING PROPER FISHING CLOTHES — Fish are constantly aware of their surroundings since it is one of the keys to their survival. If something appears on the scene that is unnatural, their instincts will alert them to flee and hide. That's why fishermen should wear clothing that blends with the background, helping to camouflage their

presence. Brightly-colored shorts and hats greatly reduce the angler's chances of being able to sneak up on a fish.

For example, you should wear the conventional khaki-colored clothing in the western part of the U.S. Or you should wear olive green in England, since the countryside is very lush and green (I learned that I caught more fish that way). For saltwater fly fishing, wear clothing that will blend in well with the background of the sky behind the boat, such as white for a cloudy day or blue when it is clear and sunny. (*Not illustrated.*)

140. USE POLAROID SUNGLASSES IN DIFFERENT COLORS — Most anglers are aware that using Polaroid glasses to eliminate glare is an essential part of seeking trout, bonefish, steelheads and other species that we actually look for before making the cast. For many years when I fished in the tropics, I thought that the brownish, amber-colored glasses, which build contrast as well as block out intense glare, were perfect for that environment. And I still think that amber is the best tint for most situations, certainly 90 percent of the time.

But now there are a number of tints available, ranging from blue/gray to medium yellow. So I have learned that it's good to have at least two other colors besides amber. When I have fished all day on snow-white bonefish flats, such as those on Christmas Island, for example, I have found that when using the amber tint my eyes became very tired. When I switched to the blue/gray color, it made such a difference. No more eye strain on bright flats! Blue/gray is also a fine color to use on the open sea. I agree with the many experienced saltwater anglers who feel that they see fish in the depths better with this color.

The medium yellow tint, similar to those used in skeet and trap shooting, is perfect for certain fishing conditions.

When fishing on smaller trout streams, where the water is often shaded and difficult to see through, I have found that the yellowish tint builds contrast. And contrast can make a world of difference in seeing fish. These glasses are also superb for darker, overcast days. Do keep in mind, however, that yellow glasses often tire the eyes on light-colored flats under a bright sun.

So if you have not tried using sunglasses with tints in a variety of colors, give them a chance — you'll increase your probability of success. (*Not illustrated.*)

141

141. TILTING THE HEAD TO SEE BETTER — Polaroid sunglasses are designed for average seeing conditions, which means there will be times when you are fishing and the sun is at such a certain angle that the glasses aren't going to get rid of all the glare. So try tilting the head one way, and then the other. Many times this simple act will assist in eliminating more glare.

142. IMPROVE YOUR VISION — In fly fishing situations where it is necessary to see the fish before casting, wearing the right kind of hat is important. Certainly any hat brim will aid vision, but you need to wear a hat with the right kind of brim.

142

Try a simple experiment. Without wearing a hat, stand on a high bank overlooking a stream and look at the bottom. Note the amount of bottom you can see. Put on a hat with a light-colored brim, and you will see more of the bottom. Now, replace the hat with one that has a dark brim, and you'll see even more of the bottom. The dark brim reduces the amount of glare that is first reflected off the water and then bounces off the brim into your eyes, reducing your vision.

To darken a brim, just apply some black liquid shoe polish to it. Be sure to allow the brim to air well before wearing, since fresh shoe polish contains eye-irritating fumes.

143. THE SOAP BOX TRICK — There are times when trout fishermen need to know what is hatching, so that a proper imitation can be presented to feeding fish. Most of us carry a net for dipping insects off the surface to examine, but carrying these nets tends to be cumbersome.

For less than a dollar, you can make a superior trap to collect insects that is easy to carry and very durable. Purchase a plastic soap box. Open it and cut away most of the bottom, leaving about 1/4-inch around the outside edge. Now cut a piece of plastic screen (the kind that is used to keep insects out of the house, available at hardware stores) to fit snugly inside the bottom of the box. Using a hot-glue gun, glue the screen to the 1/4-inch ledge that you constructed in the box.

You now have a superb insect sampler. When you want to catch insects, simply place the box in the water and let the insects wash against the screen. When ready, close the box and lift it from the water. You can even leave the insects in the box for later study or for tying imitations. The box takes up little room in the fly jacket and is very durable.

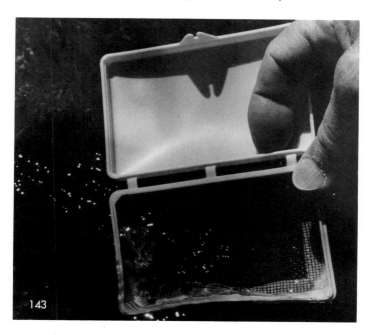

143

144. FOAM LINES — If you are new to dry fly or nymph fishing, or you are fishing streams that you have never fished before, you may wonder where to drift your fly in a pool. The best spots are easy to locate, since the upstream riffle from the pool creates foam which flows through the pool. This foam doesn't move in an even manner, but in very specific paths, which I call "food highways."

If you drift your fly along one of these food highways, you stand a much better chance of success. They are easy to locate as they flow through the pool. Don't cast your flies where foam has collected along the pool sides. Instead, offer them at the location where the foam is flowing along.

145. CHECK THOSE SPIDER WEBS — When trout fishing, it pays to know just what flies have been hatching so that you can present the proper imitation. Spiders build webs to catch insects, so we can use these to our advantage. Trees, fences, larger wild plants, and almost any large bridge near the stream often hold a spider web. Once you locate

145

one, it's pretty easy to determine which insects have recently been hatching.

146. FISH THE RIGHT ANGLE — In moving rivers, the shape of a rock often determines where the predatory fish will be hiding. In the photo, the long arrow indicates cur-

146

rent flow. The upright rock (where the short arrow points) indicates that a pocket of still water can be found immediately upstream of the rock at a right angle to the current flow. A fish will hold in such a location, because it has no swift current to battle and can see food approaching.

147. HOT SPOTS BELOW COOL DAMS — Favorite holding places for trout are below large dams which emit heavy flows of cool water that trout find enticing. Trout will also hold there to feed on tasty morsels of bait fish which are chopped up as they are forced through the dam's whirling turbines. And in the fall, when brown trout make upstream runs to their spawning sites, small dams often impede their progress, thus creating hot holding pools of trout for lucky anglers.

148. LOCATE BIG TROUT AT NIGHT — It's no secret to many top fishermen that trophy-size brown trout are basically night feeders, so finding such trout must literally be done in the dark.

If you'll purchase a powerful five-cell flashlight, you can use it to locate big browns and know exactly where they are before making your cast. Walk the stream banks of creeks you feel may hold big trout, sweeping the flashlight across the water. You'll be surprised to often find these huge fish feeding in only inches of water, often at the tail of a pool.

When you see a good fish, don't hold the light on the fish, but swing it away. If you hold it on the trout, the fish may become alarmed and swim away. Wait a bit, then sweep the light quickly back over the spot to see if the fish is still there — chances are that it will be. Then turn off the light, get into a good casting position, and offer the fish a big night fly.

149. STAY LOW — One of the most common mistakes made by fishermen is to stand upright when nearing the

fish. Because of the way that fish see things above water, upright anglers are seen better than you might realize. You will be spotted if you walk upright along a trout stream, or stand tall in a flats boat when seeking saltwater species. So anytime you get close to a fish, stay low.

For example, when in a flats boat at close range, it's wise to bend down as low as possible during the presentation.

149-A

Or when stalking trout in small streams, try to approach the water by crawling, crouching low, or best of all, hiding behind some brush to mask your approach.

Or you may want to adopt what I call the "prayer attitude," which is a great way to get into position on a small stream without being detected by fish. In fact, the sign of a good fisherman will be the worn knees on his hip boots, caused by creeping and crawling a great deal.

150. STAY IN THE SHADE — Whenever possible, stay hidden in the shade. You are less likely to be detected while in the shade as opposed to placing yourself in sunlight.

151. DON'T WARN YOUR FISH — Don't make the mistake of wading too fast in a quiet pool. The water in a pool is something like water in a balloon. If you push on

one side of the balloon, the water will shift to the other side. Anytime you wade in a pool and can see small waves radiating more than three feet from your legs, you are probably pushing shock waves of water that will alert all the fish throughout the pool. So, *always* wade as slowly as possible when moving in quiet water.

152

152. BUBBLES ARE A TARPON GIVEAWAY — It's difficult to spot small tarpon in tidal rivers and still water, unless you see them rolling or lying under the brush. However, you can figure out if they have been around recently. Tarpon frequently come to the surface, expel air, suck in fresh air, and then drop below the surface. When they come up, this expulsion of air generally leaves a trail of bubbles on the surface, which is a great fish indicator for someone who knows how to look for them.

153. ROLLERS ARE A TARPON TIP-OFF — Another way to find a tarpon is to watch out for them rolling. Tarpon can breathe air from above or right below the surface. Again,

they will push their head above water, suck in fresh air and roll toward the bottom. It is so exciting to watch an entire school of giant tarpon rolling as they approach your boat. (*Not illustrated.*)

154. WAKES GOING THE WRONG WAY — In very shallow water, fish moving below the surface create a definite small wave. If there is a series of waves or small ripples, all moving in one direction, but a single one moving against them or in a different direction, it is almost always a sign of swimming fish. So if you see a wave that seems to be going in a direction different from the normal wave action of the water, you can often locate fish at a long distance from you. (*Not illustrated.*)

155. MUDDYING RAYS — A good way of locating fish on tropical flats is to look for stingrays. Fish will often follow rays as they cruise along, so they can quickly grab small morsels that have been frightened by the ray. Frequently predator fish, such as redfish, bonefish, and mutton snappers, will even hover above rays as they are feeding. When rays feed, they settle to the bottom over a place where they believe shrimp, crabs, or other food is hidden, hovering and beating their wings against the bottom, terrorizing the creatures into fleeing out into the open. In the process, rays will unsettle a great deal of bright mud which can be spotted as it is carried away with the tide.

When you locate a ray that is muddying, throw a popping bug or streamer into the area where the mud is most dense. (*Not illustrated.*)

156. BIRDS CAN BE INDICATORS — In saltwater fishing, birds can be a sure indicator of a hot spot. When the tide ebbs, little gutters and small ditches drain the last of the

156

water, and small bait fish tend to remain in these flooded shallows as long as they can. When they must retreat to deeper water, they swim in the ditches that have been formed by the ebbing tide. Waiting for this moment, birds will congregate around the ditches hoping to pluck the hapless bait fish from the water. Predator fish will also get into the action, lying at the down tide, or outlet side, of a drainage ditch. Put a fly in there and you stand a good chance of catching one.

157. NERVOUS WATER — There is an occurrence that experienced anglers call "nervous water." This is water that has many tiny ripples on it. Perhaps most of the surface of the water is calm, excepting a small area which appears to be nervous or agitated. This agitated condition is frequently

caused by fish movement below the surface. Anytime you see such an occurrence, it's worth checking out.

158. WADING GRIT FREE — When wading bonefish flats, most people now use diving boots, or one of the new flats boot designs that are now on the market, since sneakers

allow too much grit to work its way inside. But when dirt or grit rises above the top of your footwear, even boots can't keep it out. So use gravel guards. If properly placed on the legs, they do a great job. Wear long pants and wear them on the outside of the boots. Then place the gravel guards over your pants and boots. As you are wading, dirt that filters upward will seep up and over the gravel guards and be flushed away. If grit comes down inside the gravel guards, because the pants are on the outside, the grit will be forced out of the bottom, allowing little to get into your boots.

159. SLIDE YOUR FOOT ON THE FLATS — When wading a flat for bonefish, permit, and similar species, stingrays can often be encountered. These creatures burrow into the soft bottom and are hard to see. If you step on one, the ray may strike you, imparting a bite that could put you in the hospital. But the stingray doesn't want to be stepped on and will simply flee if given a chance. So never lift your foot off the bottom when wading a flat, as shown below.

Instead, always *slide your foot along* in contact with the bottom. That way, if your foot touches a ray, it will flee and leave you unharmed.

160. WADE WITH STAFF AT THE RIGHT POSITION —
When wading in heavy water, many people position their
wading staff upstream. But if they take a fall, the current
will push them away from the staff and the support it was
providing. I recommend wading with the staff downstream
of you, so that you can rely upon it in case you slip.

161. PHOTOGRAPH THEM AT LOW TIDE OR WATER
LEVELS — Lakes and reservoirs often have their water
drained, usually during a drought, so that a good deal of the

bank is exposed. Tides create the same situation along shorelines. If you really want to know what the bottom of a lake, saltwater channel, or shoreline looks like, take pictures of it at its low-water level. To locate exactly where there are structures where fish may hide, be sure to include some landmarks in the photograph that will be visible when the water rises again.

162. THE BEST TIME TO FISH THEM — Few anglers realize it, but in the eastern U.S., limestone trout streams are fished most successfully during winter. Because there is less angling traffic, the fish are more relaxed. And since at that time there is no surface food, the fish will concentrate on any submerged food that is available.

162-A

162-B

And here's a piece of good news: you really need only two patterns in sizes 12 through 18 to catch winter trout. A fresh water shrimp pattern (shown on either side at the top of the coin in the photo above) and a scud (sow bug) pattern (shown on either side at the bottom of the coin) are all you need, since they are the major food sources for trout during the colder months.

PRESENTATIONS

163. HELPING A DRAG-FREE DRIFT — You should usually let your dry fly drift as naturally on the surface as possible. But if there are a number of conflicting currents, or you are at the tail of a pool where swifter water wants to suck the fly line and drag the fly with it, you will often need to help the drift.

Locate a log, rock or some object that you can throw the line over. This will reduce the chances of the current pulling against the line and spoiling your presentation.

164. TO CHECK THAT DRIFT — Use foam to determine if your dry fly is drifting drag-free. Toss your fly near a bit of drifting foam. If the foam and the fly start moving in opposite directions, then you are not getting a drag-free drift, and you need to repair your leader.

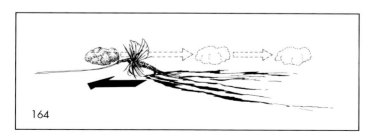

165. MOVE THAT ROD — A common mistake made by many anglers when casting across a current (tidal or fresh water), is to make the cast and leave the rod pointing in the direction of the cast. So, for example, if a river runs north to south, they cast to the northwest and leave the rod pointing northwest as the line and fly drift south with the current. As a result, a large downstream sag forms in the line between the rod tip and the fly. The farther the fly drifts, the deeper this sag accumulates in the line, causing the fly to swim unnaturally fast so that fish will generally refuse it.

A much better technique is to make the cast, and as the fly drifts with the current, keep moving the rod downstream, always attempting to keep the line as straight as possible between the rod and the fly. That way you get a better drift and have less slack in the line when you want to strike.

166. CHECK THOSE NYMPHS — When fishing for trout with nymphs, usually the fly should be drifting near the bottom, where trout feed on these morsels. Since your fly will be touching the bottom a lot, always check to make sure no debris is on the hook. Trout will refuse a fly with grass, algae or other debris on it. Also, check the hook point frequently, since points can be dulled when they drift against rocks. (*Not illustrated.*)

167. MAKING A SHORTER ROD — Short fly rods are only really useful when you fish very tight, narrow, brush-filled streams. In almost all other trout fishing situations, rods from seven and one-half to nine feet in length are preferred by almost all skilled trout fishermen.

But occasionally when using a longer rod, you might get into a tight situation where there is little casting room. So I use a little trick to "shorten" my rod that has helped me for years. Slide the rod hand up to just below the large stripping guide and make the cast. You'll see that you have effectively shortened the rod by about a foot. You'll be surprised at how easy it is to cast this way. Once the cast is made, reposition your hand to the normal fishing position.

168. DROPLETS RUIN THE PRESENTATION — It's important when making a false cast above a trout to never whip the water from your dry fly before making another presentation. If you do this on a calm surface, this act of

flushing the water will produce scores of droplets which will fall to the surface directly above the fish, scaring it away. Always dry the fly by false casting to another side, and on the final cast, drop it to the fish.

169. CASTING TO RISES — The trout sees a fly drifting on the current and it drifts back and up, then sucks in the in-

sect. It then moves forward to its feeding station. So, the fish always takes the fly off the surface downstream from where it is holding.

Don't make the mistake of casting directly to the trout as it rises to the surface, a movement indicated by a ring formed in the water. When you see a ring, try to cast two or three feet upstream from it. In that manner, the fly will float into the trout's line of vision.

170. LONG CASTS ARE VALUABLE — While most fish are caught at short range, there are times when standing well back (so you won't be detected) and making a long cast are essential for fishing success. This angler is throwing a tight loop and long line, and the smallmouths are unlikely to know he's around until it's too late.

171. THE LONG ROLL CAST — On quiet pools, if you false cast a fly line in the air, the fish might see it and flee.

This is a good time to make a long roll cast, which keeps the line close to the water and out of the fish's sight.

172. GET RID OF THAT LOOSE LINE — When casting a dry fly upstream, be sure to pay attention to the line at the rod tip, not the fly. In the photo at left below, the angler has made the mistake of letting the line drift downstream from the tip. Excess line makes it difficult to strike, and loose line will create additional drag that affects the fly's drift.

You need to continually remove all slack during the drift, as shown at right above.

173. CORRECTLY FISHING A POND OR LAKE SHORE — If you fish with the fly line traveling over land there is a good chance the back cast will snag on something.

Be sure you fish with the rod over the water so the fly line on both your back and forward casts will be over the water and out of harm's way.

174. REACH CAST FOR A DRAG-FREE DRIFT — As soon as the fly line moves downstream of the drifting fly, it begins to drag the fly in an unnatural way on the water. So use a reach cast to keep the line upstream of the fly for a more natural drift. To execute a reach cast, make a high, slow cast in the direction of the target.

As soon as forward rod motion stops, sweep the rod over and upstream as far as you can reach. Be sure to feed slack through your line hand. The entire line will fall well upstream of the fly and give you a long, drag-free drift.

175. LIGHT LINES TAKE BIGGER FISH — On a small stream or any calm water such as a quiet lake, disturbing the surface will frighten trout. In such circumstances, you'll need long leaders, at least 12 feet in length. But long leaders are difficult to cast accurately. So if you want to, instead of using a long leader, try a short leader with a very light line, sizes 2, 3, or 4. This type of line is light enough so that surface impact is reduced enough to enable you to use much shorter leaders and improve your accuracy. (*Not illustrated.*)

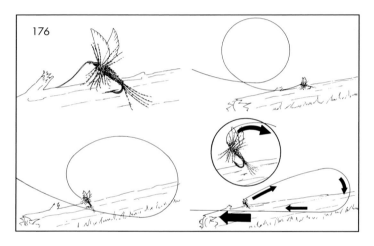

176. FLIP IT OFF BACKWARDS — If you should lodge a fly in a log or other obstruction, there is an easy trick for getting it free most of the time. Make a gentle roll cast and watch the unrolling line, and when the loop passes *beyond* whatever obstruction is holding your hook, make a hard back cast. Since the leader and front of the line are now behind the obstruction, the fly will usually free itself.

177. BE READY IN SALTWATER — Whenever you are fly fishing from a boat in saltwater, you must be ready to cast

as soon as the fish presents itself to you. To be prepared, make the longest false cast that you can. Then strip the retrieved line into a bucket. (In the photo at left below, the angler has stripped his line into the white bucket forward of his right foot.) If you use a large fly (such as is used for sailfish), it will dry out on the cast and not be in a condition to sink quickly to the fish. So place the fly in a second bucket (in the photo at left, the smaller dark bucket) containing an inch of water to keep the fly wet.

When you are running in the boat seeking fish, lay your rod on top of the large bucket. When fish are seen, pick up your rod, as well as your fly from the small bucket, and when you cast, the line will come shooting freely out of the large bucket.

178. SHOOTING BASKET THAT WORKS — Fly fishermen that work the surf soon determine that they must devise some kind of method to keep retrieved line out of the swirling water at their feet. Try this method. Cut eight or 10 three-inch lengths of 100-pound monofilament. Drill holes for each stub in the bottom of a rectangular, plastic pan like the one used for washing dishes. The holes should be slightly smaller than the diameter of the monofilament.

178

With a match, heat a ball on the end of each monofilament stub, then cut a taper on the other ends of the monofilament strands. From the bottom of the pan, shove the stubs through the holes. If you drilled the holes properly, you will have to force the stubs a bit to slide them through. Push each stub until the ball you formed with the match is seated against the pan bottom. Now, using a hot glue gun, puddle a bit of the hot glue around each ball where each stub exits into the pan.

Cut a small hole in either side at the top of the pan. Use elastic shock cord with hooks as a belt to hold the pan around your body while fishing.

179. LINE WINDING AROUND THE ROD — Everyone has had the experience of winding up their line, ready to leave the water, only to have line tangle around the rod several times as the tip wiggles in response to the force created by the winding motion your hand is making on the reel.

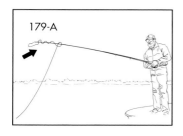
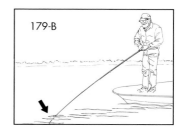

To avoid this aggravating problem, dip the rod tip under water while you are winding up, or hold it against something soft, such as grass or a person, and the tip won't wiggle.

RETRIEVING THE FLY, HOOKING UP AND PLAYING FISH

180. WHITE IS IT — When fishing nymphs, you are at a great advantage if you can see the fish. On the occasions when this happens, if you think that the nymph is somewhere near the trout and the fish makes any kind of sudden move (rolls to one side, up or down) or if you can see the white inside of its mouth — both of which are indicators that the fish has sucked in your offering — strike! (*Not illustrated.*)

181. THE RIGHT WAY TO RETRIEVE — One of the major flaws in the technique of many fly fishermen is how they go about retrieving underwater flies and popping bugs on the surface. In retrieving this type fly, you should never manipulate the fly with the rod tip. Each time you flip and then drop the rod, the slack that is created can lessen your chances of hooking a fish on the strike. An additional fault that many anglers make is to strip the line, drop it, place their hand *forward* of the hand holding the rod, and then grasp the line again. Now in order to strip again, they must

181

release the line from their rod hand and place it back in that hand again, thereby losing control of the retrieve for a brief period of time.

The retrieve should instead be made by stripping back line with the line hand. By varying the speed of the strips from slow to fast, with a pause in between, you can vary the retrieve so that the line remains taut.

Correct technique is demonstrated by the photo above. As you make your strip, bring your line hand up and *behind* the hand holding the rod and line. That way you always have control of the line.

You should also adopt this same procedure when fighting a fish. As you are recovering line, whether by reeling or stripping, always grasp the line behind your rod hand.

182. KEEP THAT ROD LOW — When fishing underwater flies or popping bugs on the surface, many anglers have the tendency to elevate the rod tip to belt level or above. This is poor technique, because when the rod is held that high, the slack that is accumulated between the rod tip and the water makes it difficult to set the hook vigorously. Also, when the rod is held high and a strong wind is blowing from one

182-A

182-B

side, as it pushes against the line and drags it sideways, the fly will continue to move, thus spoiling a good retrieve. And if the fish strikes while this is going on, there is often too much slack to set the hook well.

Better technique is to keep your rod tip as low as you can on the retrieve. I frequently even put my rod tip a few inches under the water, particularly in high wind conditions.

183. FORM AN "O" RING — Anytime line is being pulled freely and rapidly through the guides by an escaping fish, form this "O" ring with your fingers, as if it were a large ring guide, to keep the line under control.

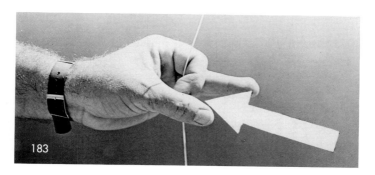

183

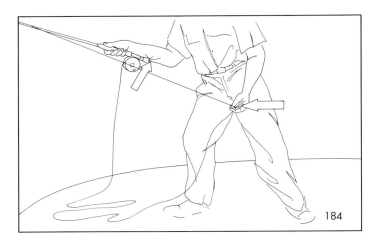

184

184. ON THE STRIKE — When a fast running fish is hooked, it is critical to immediately take control of escaping line so that you don't cause any abrupt stops that will break off the fly or tippet. So watch the line on the water or deck, making certain that as it streaks through the guides it doesn't tangle. Then jam the butt of the fly rod against the forearm (as shown in the illustration), which will eliminate the possibility of escaping line catching behind the rod handle and causing an abrupt stop and break-off.

185. TURN THE ROD UPSIDE DOWN — When a powerful fish is running and the line is being pulled through the guides, it will frequently form a knot that can jam in the snake guides. In these situations, the line will almost always go through the first two guides easily. But when the rod tip bends, the line won't continue to follow closely parallel to the rod blank, but will instead push against the outside wire edges of the snake guides. As it does, if a knot has been formed in the line, it will frequently get caught on the wire of the guides, causing the leader to break.

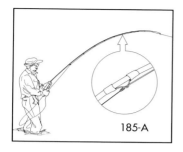
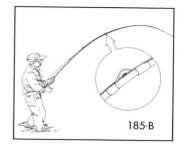

185-A   185-B

To prevent this, hold the rod upside down when you see a knot approaching the guides. In this way, unless the knot is unusually large, it will travel along the rod blank and generally squeeze through.

186. REVERSE THE REEL — On some fly reels, the drag is on the opposite side of the handle, so that during a fight with a large fish, if the angler needs to adjust the drag, it can be a difficult task to execute. But if the rod is rotated 180 degrees, the handle will now be positioned on the opposite side of the rod hand, and the drag can be easily adjusted with the line hand. Simply reach down, make the adjustment, and then rotate the rod back to its proper position. One caution: don't forget to turn the drag adjustment in the proper direction!

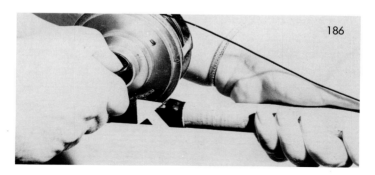

186

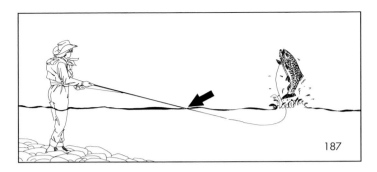

187

187. DIPPING TO LEAPERS — While a fish can create a strong force when it swims directly away from the angler; at any other angle water resistance will weaken its movements. Thus, a fish shaking its head to rid itself of your fly is not going to be able to create many severe jolts on your line while it is underwater.

But when the fish rises above the surface, it is in a position to thrust its full weight against the leader. And if the hook is not solidly imbedded in its mouth, or you're using a fragile leader, the fish will often escape. To solve this problem, you need to create slack in the leader and line *while the fish is in the air.*

I think dipping the rod is the best way to do this. When the fish rises in the air, immediately point the rod toward the fish and dip the tip into the water. By dipping the rod underwater in the direction of the fish, you will produce slack that can be controlled. With the more traditional way of bowing to a fish, loose slack gets formed and entangled on the rod tip or around the fish, and the game is lost.

188. PUMP AND WIND — With any strong fish, never try to bring it in by winding the reel handle. Instead, pump and wind. By lifting the rod, you draw the fish toward you. Lower the rod and retrieve line. *Keep a slight bend in the rod*

188

as you lower it, or you may create slack and lose your fish. Then repeat the pump and wind operation. Incidentally, never raise the rod farther than shown in the illustration, since long pumping motions are inefficient.

189. DIP THE ROD — If a fish runs under the boat, it can pull the rod against the side and break it, or tangle the line

189

in the motor or anchor line. Anytime this happens, submerge the rod, as shown, and sweep it around to the other side of the boat where you can again freely fight the fish.

190. NO STRINGS — After you have spent several thousand dollars on a tarpon fishing trip, you could blow your whole trip by not spending just a few more dollars to purchase shoes without shoestrings. Shoestrings that snag the line as it is shot toward the fish have saved many tarpon from hours of labor! If you insist upon wearing shoes (a good idea), the best kind are those that have no strings: the slip-on types. (*Not illustrated.*)

CAPTURING AND RELEASING FISH

191. DON'T TOUCH — When you catch almost any small trout, it is not really necessary to handle the fish in order to release it. To quickly remove a small fish, slide the hand

down the leader tippet until you are within two or three inches of the fish, which will allow you to hold the fish in position fairly well. Then, securely grasp the inside bend of the hook with a pair of hemostats. Using the hemostats, turn the hook up so that the point is directed toward the water. The fish's weight will now cause it to slip free of the hook. This procedure should only take seconds.

192. THREE WAYS TO IMMOBILIZE A FISH — Though it is best when releasing a fish not to touch it, there are times when it's necessary. There are several ways to do it:

192-A

Upside down — Simply hold the fish gently with its belly up and its back lying in the hand. When held upside down, the fish becomes temporarily paralyzed, at which point the hook can be removed and the fish released (192-A).

Comfort Lift — When you need to lift a fish into a boat and don't want to use a net or gaff, bring the fish along the side of the boat and slip your hand under the body where the weight is centered, usually just a short distance back from the gill cover. With your hand in this position, lift the fish from the water. Note that the fish will drape downward on either side of the hand and lie perfectly motionless. This technique works on any fish you have the strength to lift from the water — from barracudas to steelheads (192-B).

192-B

192-C

Belly Lift — Any small fish that has serious spines on the back (such as bream and panfish) should be held by the belly, where there are fewer spines (192-C).

193. A BETTER WAY TO REVIVE FISH — Most people hold a fish head-first into the current when trying to revive it. They may have good intentions, but this is not the best way to revive fish. If the fish doesn't have sharp teeth, try this method. Grip the lower jaw (which will force the mouth open) and grasp the fish firmly in front of the tail. Then rock the fish back and forth. The backward rocking motion will cause its gills to flare outward. Now, with its mouth held open, large volumes of oxygen-rich water will be forced across the gills. With this method, I have even revived fish that my fishing companions had given up on.

193

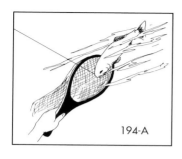
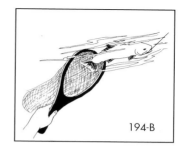

194-A

194-B

194. RIGHT AND WRONG WAYS TO NET FISH — The illustration on the left above shows the proper way to net a fish. Keep the net in one position and make sure that the fish is brought into the net *head-first*. Never try to chase or catch a fish from behind with a landing net (as shown on the right above).

195. TAILERS ARE KIND TO FISH — Many years ago European salmon fishermen developed a tailer (a handle with a steel snare on the end) to land exhausted fish quickly. This tool works on any slender fish. When the tailer is slipped over the tail, a quick yank will cause it to grip the fish faster than the eye can see. It rarely harms the fish and is certainly to be preferred over a gaff. Be careful not to slip the tailer loop over the head, since your leader will be in the way. *(Not illustrated.)*

196. MEASURE WITH A BILL — The U.S. dollar bill is just a fraction more than six inches in length (actually exactly 6 and 1/8 inches). So if you want to know how big that fish really is, one or two bills can help you measure it.

With a dollar bill, you can measure fish, a long fly, a rod handle, a fly box, or a host of other things. You can even wrap several bills around a fish to make a circular measurement of its girth. *(Not illustrated.)*

197. BEFORE AND AFTER PHOTOGRAPHS — When taking photographs, here are three situations where the position of the camera or your subject are critical:

To Bring Action into the Photo — This top photo below looks odd because the angler is positioned to the right, which makes it look as though he is fishing *outside* the camera's eye. Even if the angler had been centered in the photograph, the impression would be the same.

So always have the action move with the photo. In the bottom photo, because the photographer moved the camera's angle to the right, the angler now looks as if he were fishing into the picture. Whenever a boat is moving across the water or any action is taking place, have the subject of the picture moving or facing towards the action.

To Avoid Optical Distortion — In the photo at left below, it appears that this fellow is holding a bass that is pretty small. But it's only an optical illusion. Actually, the fish is larger than it looks. But, note that the fish is being held on the side of the angler that is farthest away from the photographer.

In the photo at right, the fish appears larger. Instead this time the angler has simply moved the fish to his other side, towards the photographer. So if you want to stay friends with your photographic models, remember which side to keep their fish on!

To Capture Lifelike Action — As shown at the top of the next page, this type of photo is most often taken of a person fly casting. He is standing upright and obviously having his picture taken, not really fishing.

But notice the difference in this photograph directly above. Now this fellow looks like he is fishing! If you'll have your subject crouch a little or put a little action into his body as he casts, the picture will look genuine.

198. BETTER PHOTOGRAPHS — Whenever you photograph several people engaged in an activity, make sure that *everyone* is looking at the center of interest. If one of these people were looking away, anyone viewing the picture would wonder what that person was looking at.

199. CAPTURING FLY LINE — When taking pictures of someone fly casting, the very best speed to capture the fly

line is at 1/250 of a second. Shoot any faster and the line will not be as large in the photo, or shoot any slower and the line will be blurred. Also, it helps to have a dark background with a light-colored line.

200. THE SILHOUETTE PHOTOGRAPH— The silhouette is a popular photograph and easy to shoot. Put the camera on manual and make a meter reading from the brightest area around the subject, which in this photograph is the sky. Then shoot that picture. If you've metered it correctly, the subject will appear totally black. If you're using an automatic camera, point it at the background, depress and continue to hold the shutter release, and then release to shoot.

200

INDEX